The Faber Book of
Twentieth-Century Women's Poetry

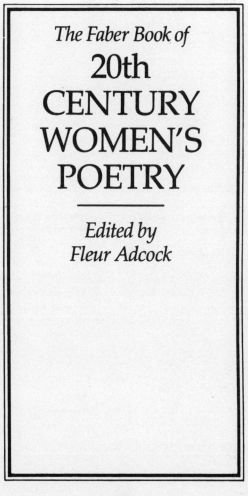

The Faber Book of
20th
CENTURY
WOMEN'S
POETRY

Edited by
Fleur Adcock

faber and faber
LONDON · BOSTON

First published in 1987 by
Faber and Faber Limited
3 Queen Square London WC1N 3AU

Photoset by Wilmaset Birkenhead Wirral
Printed in England by Mackays of Chatham PLC,
Chatham, Kent

The acknowledgements on pp. 325-30 constitute an
extension of this copyright notice.

A CIP record for this book
is available from the British Library

ISBN 0-571-13693-1

14 16 18 20 19 17 15 13

Contents

[vii]

ROBIN HYDE   1906–1939

E. J. SCOVELL   1907–

ELIZABETH BISHOP   1911–1979

JOSEPHINE MILES   1911–1985

AMY CLAMPITT 1920–

ROSEMARY DOBSON 1920–

BARBARA GUEST 1920–

GWEN HARWOOD 1920–

DENISE LEVERTOV 1923–

ELIZABETH BARTLETT 1924–

PATRICIA BEER 1924–

JANE COOPER 1924–

LAURIS EDMOND 1924–

MAXINE KUMIN 1925–

ELIZABETH JENNINGS 1926–

ANNE SZUMIGALSKI 1926–

MOLLY HOLDEN 1927–1981

CONNIE BENSLEY 1929–

FREDA DOWNIE 1929–

ANNE STEVENSON   1933–

FLEUR ADCOCK   1934–

JEAN VALENTINE   1934–

JUNE JORDAN   1936–

JUDITH RODRIGUEZ   1936–

CONTENTS

Introduction

My aim in this book has been not to illustrate a thesis or propound a view but to show how many good and interesting women poets have been writing in English during the course of this century. If I have a theory about the tradition informing their poetry it is that there is no particular tradition: there have been poets, and they have been individuals, and a few of them have influenced a few others, but on the whole there is no clear thread. This is quite natural. No one pretends that poetry in general has shown one single line of development throughout the twentieth century; if 'women's poetry' were a special genre, a minor and recognizably different offshoot from the main process, it might make sense to see it as a unity, but as things are, women have been involved in the currents and movements as little or as much as men, and have been as various.

What is different about poetry by women, of course, is not its nature but the fact that until recently it has been undervalued and to some extent neglected. Now that this phase is over (as far as at least one large section of the reading public is concerned) the reasons for it seem almost too well known to need rehearsing, but I shall summarize them in a few brief over-simplifications. They are: The publishing world was dominated by men. Editors, publishers and critics were usually male. Men tend not to take women seriously. Women as a result tended not to take themselves seriously enough, and were in any case usually too busy, too oppressed or too under-educated to write. 'Poet' was a masculine word. The Muse was female, the poet was male. There was a deep-seated conviction that women couldn't do it.

A lot of women *were* doing it, but they tended to be socially isolated, and their writing was often achieved at the cost of other satisfactions, such as family life: Charlotte Mew lived quietly with her sister (and committed suicide after the sister's death); Marianne Moore lived quietly with her mother, as did Stevie Smith with her aunt; H.D. moved for a while in a high-powered London literary circle which included Ezra Pound and D. H.

Lawrence, but after a broken marriage and other miseries she was rescued by the woman writer Bryher (Winifred Ellerman) and taken to live quietly in Switzerland.

These are women whose work at least got published. We do not know how many women poets deserved to be published but were not, and not all of those who were received anything like their due. If they did become well known it was sometimes for the wrong reasons: among those whose books actually sold, Elinor Wylie was a well-connected American society beauty who caused a headline scandal by leaving her husband and child and running off with a married man; Edna St Vincent Millay led a 'bohemian' life and wrote sexually daring poems (good poems, quite often: like Wylie she was a highly competent verse technician, but in Millay's case there was rather more beneath the surface polish of the work). Edith Sitwell was a loud self-publicist with the confidence of her aristocratic background.

These are names from what sound like remote eras of this fast-moving century. The situation now is quite different. Even if male critics and editors continue to dismiss women's poetry (and many of them do), women themselves want to read it, and there are not only women's presses but also general publishing houses which want to publish it. The fact that this anthology is appearing at all, and that it is one of a number (each with a quite different focus) to appear recently, is evidence of this. But the problem now seems to me to have shifted to a new area. The danger is that women's poetry will be shunted into a ghetto, occupying the 'Women's' section of the bookshop rather than the poetry section, and taught in 'Women's Studies' courses at universities rather than literature courses. Part of this could be blamed on women themselves, or on certain women writers, who take a radically separatist attitude, rejecting 'patriarchal standards' and 'the language of the oppressors', claiming that men do not understand the tones of voice in which women express them-selves, and addressing their work exclusively to other women. This is an inevitable stage of the social revolution, but it is hardly surprising that it antagonizes men and prejudices them against

[2]

even those women who, like most real poets, address themselves
to both sexes or to an audience which they have not attempted to
define at all.

I have set out to present here a healthy sample of poets whose
work is capable of being appreciated on its own merits. The
history of their critical and popular reputations shows a wide
variation. Some of the older contributors (Charlotte Mew, Anna
Wickham, H.D.) have recently been reassessed and have
appeared in new editions – part of the welcome and continuing
process of the rehabilitation of women writers. But others never
suffered even temporary eclipse: it would be wrong to adopt the
conspiracy theory and suggest that wholesale repression of
women's poetry has taken place in this century. Marianne
Moore, for example, was treated with respect from quite an early
stage in her career, when she was recognized by Pound and Eliot.
Later in her long life she became a public pet; the Ford Motor
Company asked her to name their latest car, and she was
featured in *Life* magazine on a visit to the zoo.

This last incident typifies a popular misreading of what she was
up to in her poems. True, she wrote about animals and other
inhabitants of the natural world with a startling and at times
outlandish vividness of perception – her subject at university was
biology, and the habits of precise observation this instilled in her
were in keeping with her own analytical temperament – but in
her poetry the brilliantly accurate descriptions are often subor-
dinated to a moral purpose. 'The Pangolin' is about courage – a
quality she often praised – and about modesty, non-aggressive-
ness and the correct use of strength; 'To a Snail' once again refers
to modesty, drawing an analogy with compression in literary
style; 'The Jerboa' touches on, among other things, the conspi-
cuous parading of grandiose wealth in contrast to the capacity to
be satisfied with very little. The uneven, unpredictable leaps of
the animal in this poem may seem to configure the dizzying
agility with which Moore's imagination leaps from one topic or
detail to another. Questions of human psychology and moral
principle are never far beneath the surface of her poems, but the

incidental delight afforded by her creatures, objects and scenes is a large part of their attraction.

Marianne Moore was one of the few women poets of her time who exerted a noticeable influence on others. Her most talented disciple was Elizabeth Bishop: the friendship between the two poets is described in Bishop's endearing and entertaining essay 'Efforts of Affection: a memoir of Marianne Moore' (included in her *Collected Prose*, 1984), where she reveals among other things (such as that Moore censored the indelicate expression 'water closet' from one of Bishop's poems) the fact that it was through the sponsorship of this older mentor that she first got into print, outside magazines.

The literary relationship between these two highly individual writers was not straightforward. They shared a concern for precision and accuracy of detail, and both were tirelessly scrupulous revisers of their own work, but they were aiming at different kinds of perfection and their minds worked in quite different ways. Moore's poem 'The Fish' takes its name simply from its opening words, and is actually about something else; Bishop's poem of the same title is about a very definite and specific fish. In her poetry things are described for their own sakes, with no obvious nudging of the reader to share an attitude or make a judgement. She can be more genuinely impersonal than Moore, effacing herself from scenes at which she is ostensibly present as narrator; and the narrative voice is sometimes that of a child – either an actual child, real or imagined (as in 'First Death in Nova Scotia'), or someone with a child's directness and lack of interest in analysis. This can be disconcerting, as can the transparent plainness of her style in poems such as 'In the Waiting Room': if this is a good poem (as I believe it is), why is it good? One reason is an apparently negative one: there is nothing wrong with it, nothing out of place or badly expressed; everything is exactly as it should be (infinitely harder to achieve than it looks). Another is that it introduces an enormous sense of almost mystical strangeness into a superficially banal setting – whereas in 'Arrival at Santos' the reverse happens, and a scene which we might have expected to be exotic is presented in terms of the ordinary and everyday (soap, postage stamps); there is a constant traffic between the strange and the familiar in Bishop's work. She spent much of her life travelling, and lived abroad a good deal, settling for many years in Brazil. The titles of her books – *North and South, Questions of Travel, Geography III* – reflect her concern with places, and the cool, contained, transportable self she took on her journeys expressed itself in the deceptively flat, calm tone of her poems; the scenes she described may pretend to be ordinary, but they make us want to look at them again.

She and Moore are both important poets, and occupy a proportionate amount of space in this anthology. Another is Sylvia Plath, who may seem to have little in common with them apart from the fact that she too was a perfectionist. Her early work shows a good many influences (this is true of most apprentice work, but hers was more publishable than some). However, by the time she came to write the poems of her maturity, often under intense pressures of anguish and despair, she had the technical ability to transform her emotions and experiences into literature and not just 'self-expression'. Her lurid, flickering images seem to come straight off the subconscious, and indeed that is the source of their power, but they have been filtered through a rigorously trained mind. The most extreme of her poems get as close to the tones of delirium or madness as it is possible for poems to go without turning into something other than poetry. To call them 'confessional' is misleading: they do not so much relate the details of her biography as zoom in on occasional states of crisis which arose from her own circumstances but have a more general significance. The name of her last poem, 'Edge', is that of the area she came to inhabit in her writing: the precarious border of endurance.

Plath, Moore and Bishop all happened to be American. The only British poet to whom I have given a comparable amount of space is Stevie Smith, whose apparently artless, casually-constructed poems might suggest a theory about a British tradition of amateurism as opposed to American professionalism if Stevie Smith were typical of anything but herself. (Certainly British poets are far less likely than American ones to be attached to the literature departments of universities, but that is not relevant here: none of the three Americans I have been discussing was a campus poet.) Stevie Smith was not as naïve as the personae of her poems are often made to sound, but she does tend to give the impression of having achieved her effects through instinct. (Instinct, she might have said, is another name for the Muse.) Her ramshackle metres and eccentric-English-lady tone, her weird, heartless little fables with their lonely, deluded or ridiculous characters, her fond but disillusioned broodings over religion and friendly familiarity towards death, give her poems the air of inspired dabblings. Perhaps she cultivated this, but for all her freakish humour she was a serious writer. Sylvia Plath admired her work, describing herself in a fan-letter as 'a desperate Smith-addict'.

Charlotte Mew, the earliest poet included here, also dwelt on death in her poetry. Two of her younger brothers died when she was a child, and her oldest brother died insane when she was in her thirties, and was buried in Nunhead Cemetery. Her poem with this title is fiction, written from the viewpoint of a young man at his fiancée's grave, half mad with grief, but it is true to her own emotions in several ways: one of the Mew sisters was also schizophrenic; Charlotte and the other sister lived in dread of insanity and vowed never to marry, but in any case Charlotte's passions (which she had to repress) were directed towards women, as is hinted in the poems I have chosen. She was not a prolific poet, but the intensity of her language and her unusually flexible handling of rhythm and metre make her work both modern enough and exciting enough to stand fitly at the opening of this volume.

I have glanced at a few of the more prominent figures in a richly crowded field. This century has produced many hundreds of women poets writing in English (let alone in other languages, which are not my province here). I have therefore had to be cruelly selective. As my intention is to some extent historical I have concentrated on not leaving too many gaps in the earlier parts of the century rather than on filling in its most recent decades; it would be impossible to do justice to the merits of all the newer or younger poets in a collection which begins with Charlotte Mew and covers more than eighty years.

Justice is what I had in mind, but it has inevitably had to be compromised. Because my space was so limited I made the somewhat arbitrary decision to include no one born later than 1945. This, like any other restriction I might have imposed, has given rise to anomalies: some of the poets under forty whom I should have liked to include have been publishing longer than certain older ones who managed to slip in under the age-bar, and many of the poems in the later pages of the anthology are fairly recent; that their authors' dates of birth happened to qualify them for entry was simply a matter of luck.

Another factor which, however regrettably, tends to operate against justice is fashion. Poetry dates, and, as with clothes, a recently outmoded style is less acceptable than an antiquated one whose time has almost come again. It is not easy now to summon a great deal of enthusiasm for the more well-mannered, ladylike poets of the 1920s, 1930s and 1940s, such as Yeats's favourite Dorothy Wellesley (although my inclusion of Ursula Bethell, Frances Cornford and others is evidence that I think we should overcome this natural prejudice and not dismiss them all).

Some, of course, were already old fashioned even when they were writing: Vita Sackville-West described herself as 'a damned outmoded poet', and in spite of her occasional felicities I have had to accept her verdict and exclude her. Others have dated for a reason which at first sight seems paradoxical (and which is also not unknown in the rag trade): that they went to the other extreme and tried too desperately to be novel. Mina Loy, a pioneer of international Modernism, was praised by Eliot and Pound, but these and her more recent advocates have failed to persuade me that her 'poetry of ideas and wordplay' retains much more than curiosity value; her impulse to experiment was admirable in itself, but the results now look almost as quaint and over written as Sackville-West's Miltonic or Virgilian imitations.

Other experimentalists have been more successful and more durable. Marianne Moore stands out as genuinely original, not only by reason of her technical innovations (the syllabic lines, the idiosyncratically shaped stanzas, the use of appliquéed prose quotations) but in the way she compels apparently intractable material, jagged with scientific terms and abstruse locutions, into elegant, witty statements. Her style is all her own: unlike Loy, who was influenced by Laforgue and a bundle of others, she developed it by herself. Laura Riding is another authentic innovator but unfortunately her work cannot be shown in the context of this anthology because she does not allow it to appear in any book which separates work by gender. Gertrude Stein, on the other hand, has been omitted, on the grounds that her true medium was prose, not poetry.

Then there are the borderline cases, those whose apparent originality went little deeper than surface tricks. Edith Sitwell was convinced, and convinced others (Yeats among them), that she had introduced a new note into English literature. Her games with sound, her dance-tune rhythms, her use of nonsense-rhymes and synaesthesia, and her whole clutter of literary/historical/mythological/folkloric paraphernalia enhanced the entertainment value of the Sitwell circus, but it is as entertainment that they must now be chiefly viewed. The package as a whole was new, but the individual elements remained insufficiently transformed to constitute a major poetry. Sitwell deserves to be remembered, though, if only because for years she inscribed on the popular consciousness an image of what 'modern poetry' was. Her early work was her liveliest and most attractive; I have represented her by a small sample of it.

Elizabeth Daryush, a less publicly visible figure, also earns a modest place. Her experiments with syllabic verse were of interest, but unfortunately she disguised their novelty in a diction which was almost as archaic as that of her father, Robert Bridges.

Technical innovation, or the appearance of it, can be deceptive. In any case it is not all we require of poetry: plenty of good poets have been able to speak in new ways or address new subjects within the existing prosodic conventions of their time – whatever time that happened to be.

Here I should say something about my decision to arrange the poets chronologically by date of birth. There is no ideal way of organizing a mixed collection of work such as this, in which so many styles, traditions and national or regional characteristics run parallel or intersect. A grouping by country would have reduced the book to a series of mini-anthologies (plus a few floating individuals with qualifications for more than one nationality) without necessarily revealing the ways in which currents of influence have flowed around the world (sometimes sluggishly, often unpredictably) between one literature and another. The most historically satisfying method, perhaps, would have been to arrange every poem by date of composition or first publication, but this impossibly pedantic procedure would have broken up each author's body of work. Arrangement by theme is equally disruptive, and also artificial. The various other possible permutations of chronological, geographical and thematic order which might suggest themselves to a truly ingenious editor would no doubt reveal more meaningful links between one poet and another than does my straightforward date-of-birth system, but at least the latter points up the fact I want to emphasize: the great variety of styles in which women poets are writing and have written. I like to imagine a series of slight, pleasurable shocks tingling through the unprepared reader who comes upon such different poets as Frances Bellerby, Stevie Smith and Lorine Niedecker in quick succession.

One of several pieces of information which date-of-birth order conceals, though, is the publishing history of the poets: two women born in the same year may have published their first collections ten, twenty, or even thirty years apart. I suspect that this factor would be less pronounced in an anthology which included men: late development as a poet, or at any rate delayed publication, seems to be a predominantly female phenomenon. If we look only at the first two poets in my list of contents, Charlotte Mew, born in 1869, published her first book in 1916; Ursula Bethell, born in 1874, published hers in 1929, and had not even begun seriously writing poetry until after the age of fifty. Their immediate successors were more precocious, but among poets born in the 1920s there is a recurrence of the delayed-appearance syndrome: Gwen Harwood, Elizabeth Bartlett, Lauris Edmond, Connie Bensley, Freda Downie and U. A. Fanthorpe all published their first collections when they were over forty, and in some cases over fifty; to take an extreme example, Amy Clampitt, born in 1920, did not publish her first poem until 1978, when she emerged suddenly as a highly sophisticated poet with a fully developed style, and her first commercial book appeared only in 1983. (It was well worth waiting for.)

So what happened? Were they late starters or just slow developers? Were they too distracted by domestic responsibilities to begin writing early? Did they lack confidence? Was their poetry rejected? There has been much illuminating discussion of these questions in recent years: see, for example, Tillie Olsen's book *Silences* (Virago, 1980), Joanna Russ's *How to Suppress Women's Writing* (The Women's Press, 1984), and Jane Cooper's examination of her own case in the essay included together with her poems in *Scaffolding* (Anvil Press, 1984). But such studies cannot answer for all the individual women I have mentioned, or explain why things were different for them than for their contemporaries. Unless we are told we can only guess. Ursula Bethell, for example, was apparently not prevented from writing: she was unmarried and not overwhelmed by family duties; she travelled abroad, she did welfare work during the First World War, and after she had returned to New Zealand the poetry began. She seems simply to have waited until she was ready.

In other cases there were no doubt difficulties or setbacks, but these can occur in any life (for men too). The only generalization I would risk is that women seem particularly unwilling to be discouraged from writing, however late it may be getting. Now that the social and literary climate has become more receptive to poetry by women it is being written not only by the young but by women in whom the poetic faculty had lain dormant, or been suppressed, for years. Jane Cooper was asked, during her attempt to understand in retrospect why she had felt obliged to give up poetry for a long period in her youth, 'Didn't anyone ever tell you it was all right to write?' 'Yes, but not to be a writer,' she replied. In the last ten or fifteen years many more women have been discovering that it is 'all right' to be poets. I find this enormously encouraging.

Every anthologist runs up against the problem of 'anthology pieces' – poems which stand out from an author's work, stand well alone, and seem ideally designed to go into an anthology. This often means that they have already been in one: it is maddening to find, after faithfully sifting a poet's entire work, that the poems one prefers are those which previous anthologists have likewise favoured. Time after time I have gleefully picked out *different* poems by a particular poet, only to discard them one by one when forced to make the final choice. In such cases the best solution is to give in and use the obvious candidates; after all, they will not be obvious to everyone: not many people outside New Zealand, for example, will know that a certain poem by Robin Hyde or Ursula Bethell has been chosen before, and if it is a good poem it deserves to be read again.

This is a trivial aspect of a wider subject, and one which raises the possibility of real injustice. Some poets write potential 'anthology pieces' (striking, self-contained, and often short) nearly all the time: I could happily have filled twice as many pages with the work of Josephine Miles, for example. With others the opposite is the case: to represent them fairly one would need to offer a large body of work or at least one very long poem, and their poetry does not lend itself easily to being excerpted. Denise Levertov has written of her concept of 'organic poetry', in which 'the peculiar rhythms of the parts are modified, if necessary, in order to discover the rhythms of the whole'. This could apply to her poem 'Matins', which would

[11]

lose its force and its connections if cut up into anthology-sized chunks. I have included the whole of 'Matins', but there are other poems, by this and other poets, which I have had either to omit or to damage by amputation.

One poet who presents such a problem is H.D. She used to be classed as an Imagist and known principally for the short, concentrated poems she wrote during her association with Pound before World War I and for the classically influenced lyrics which followed them; but her style altered over the years, and her most substantial work is now seen to be the epic poems she wrote much later, and particularly her *Trilogy*. The first part of this, *The Walls Do Not Fall*, was written in London during World War II, and the rest soon afterwards. I was tempted to offer extracts from the second section, *Tribute to the Angels*, but as soon as I began interfering with the fabric of it the whole thing seemed to unravel into loose threads of mysticism and arcane allusion, and the carefully built up atmosphere of the poem evaporated. It works as a unity, but only as that.

Poets who write in this way, concentrating on the total effect rather than the tidy rounding-off of each part, lay themselves open to charges of technical incompetence or indifference. 'It has a certain raw power, but where are the line-endings?' said a male poet to whom I showed some recent work by Adrienne Rich. One answer to this, which I was not quick enough to give at the time, should have been: 'In her early work, in poems such as 'Aunt Jennifer's Tigers', written before her style evolved into something more open.'

Rich is generally recognized as the poet who has most roundly and significantly expressed women's feelings about their sexual identity and their value in society. It may be said that she goes to extremes: the world of her recent poetry is almost the obverse equivalent of the monastic settlements on Mount Athos, where the monks are said to ban all female creatures and go without eggs rather than admit a hen; for Rich only female animals are of interest – every lion must be a lioness, every dog a bitch. This is a forgivable quirk, but the attitude it represents means that literary considerations get pushed aside under the pressure of political rage. Her by now classic poem 'Snapshots of a Daughter-in-Law' belongs to the transitional period between her early academicism and her present style; it is a successful piece of work, well constructed without being too formal, but she has since written 'It strikes me now as too literary, too dependent on allusion; I hadn't found the courage yet to do without authorities . . .' I cannot share the view that to write truly as a woman one must reject literary traditions merely because they were largely forged by men (which seems as short-sighted as to reject printed books, motor-cars and antibiotics because men invented them), but I respect Rich's work and have tried to give some idea, through a few brief selections, of the stages through which it has progressed.

I should like to be able to say, as Marianne Moore did on an otherwise blank page at the front of her *Complete Poems*, 'Omissions are not accidents'; but that would be untrue. Apart from the omissions which have been imposed on me by lack of space, and a few more which I somewhat reluctantly imposed on myself, it is inevitable that I must inadvertently have missed not only poems but entire poets. Some omissions, though, are not accidental. Anne Sexton, for example, is not here: in the past I read her work with sympathy, but it now strikes me as excessively derivative (first from Lowell, then from Plath) and repellently self-indulgent. (Possibly she is a victim of the swings of fashion: 1960s confessional is not a style to which the 1980s reader easily warms.) Other poets, still living, share the same taint. Sylvia Plath has been innocently responsible for a mob of more or less feeble imitators: powerfully individual poets usually make bad models.

Naturally I have prejudices. I am not interested in 'primal scream' writing: slabs of raw experience untransformed by any attempt at ordering and selection. I am bewildered and after a time bored by the profusion of careful, sensitive cryptic minimalists who have emerged from the Creative Writing Programs of the American universities (which is not to say that some distinctively recognizable poets have not taken the same path). I am not attracted to incantatory poetry – or not, at least, to poetry which is that and nothing more: incantation can have its place in a poem, as can any other rhythmical technique, but a collection consisting entirely of chants, charms, spells, prayers and other forms of heightened utterance usually turns out to be lazy writing and short on sense. Even poets who are not usually silly can get carried away by 'beauty' of sound and skid dangerously close to this condition.

Rhythm is of course crucial in poetry, the one essential factor which distinguishes a poem from a set of observations or notes; but a true sense of rhythm embraces variability and sensitivity to the relation between sound and content. It is a subtle, elusive quality, publicly transmitted through the written word and yet intimately personal in its derivation from the poet's own speaking voice. It can be tracked throughout the course of this collection in a protean multiplicity of incarnations, from the disturbing metrical shifts and deliberately not-quite-regular stanzas of Charlotte Mew through Stevie Smith's seductively off-key conversational sing-song to the cool, mysterious, delicately controlled flow of Louise Glück's lines.

What I like should be evident from my choices. I enjoy the odd or unexpected: not surrealism (a tired old tradition by now, and surely never one which was as much fun for its readers as for its practitioners) but the kind of detail which throws new and startling light on some facet of what actually exists or could exist. Stevie Smith is full of it; so is Sylvia Plath, with her extraordinary images; then there is Elizabeth Bishop – I think of her singing Baptist hymns to a seal, 'like me a believer in total immersion', in 'At the Fishhouses'; and May Swenson's 'pretend' horse cropping real clover in 'The Centaur'; and, unforgettably, Marianne Moore's 'imaginary gardens with real toads in them' – a metaphor for poetry which she herself came to reject, when she revised the poem called 'Poetry', but which I, together with most of her admirers, have refused to relinquish.

One word for all this is 'imagination'; or you could call it 'originality', or perhaps 'illumination': a kind of sparkle. Often it is a matter of tone as much as of detail, and is related to another quality I admire: wit. This is a characteristic of all the poets represented here at some length – Moore, Smith, Bishop, Plath (even in the last despairing weeks of her life it persisted, although often blackly) – and of Miles, Beer, Kumin, Szumigalski, Fanthorpe, and many others. Sometimes (as with Wendy Cope) it takes the form of actual comic writing, a rather different and more specialized use of linguistic and tonal ingenuity. Wit should not, and in good poets does not, conflict with seriousness and humanity: it tends rather to enhance them. When we read poetry we want to be moved, surprised, entertained and convinced; if all these effects are achieved by the same poem, so much the better.

Although the contents of this book are of my own choosing and must inevitably reflect my taste, I have tried not to be too dominated by personal preferences but to pay attention to poetry in styles which I did not find immediately sympathetic. In the course of my reading I made discoveries and underwent conversions. One of the less fortunate side-effects of this was that poets who were on my original list sometimes got pushed out to make way for others, with the result that for me the book is now haunted by the phantoms of poems which nearly made it but disappeared in the final revisions. (I should perhaps add that the poems of my own which are included went in at the same late stage, at the insistence of my Faber editor, Craig Raine.)

In any case, no anthology which includes the work of living poets can be anything but provisional. This one is merely an introduction to the work of the poets it presents, not a substitute for reading their books.

CHARLOTTE MEW

The Farmer's Bride

Three Summers since I chose a maid,
Too young maybe – but more's to do
At harvest-time than bide and woo.
  When us was wed she turned afraid
Of love and me and all things human;
Like the shut of a winter's day.
Her smile went out, and 'twasn't a woman –
  More like a little frightened fay.
    One night, in the Fall, she runned away.

'Out 'mong the sheep, her be,' they said,
'Should properly have been abed;
But sure enough she wasn't there
Lying awake with her wide brown stare.
So over seven-acre field and up-along across the down
  We chased her, flying like a hare
Before our lanterns. To Church-Town
  All in a shiver and a scare
We caught her, fetched her home at last
  And turned the key upon her, fast.

She does the work about the house
As well as most, but like a mouse:
  Happy enough to chat and play
  With birds and rabbits and such as they,
  So long as men-folk keep away.
'Not near, not near!' her eyes beseech
When one of us comes within reach.
  The women say that beasts in stall
  Look round like children at her call.
  I've hardly heard her speak at all.

[17]

Shy as a leveret, swift as he,
Straight and slight as a young larch tree,
Sweet as the first wild violets, she,
To her wild self. But what to me?

The short days shorten and the oaks are brown,
    The blue smoke rises to the low grey sky,
One leaf in the still air falls slowly down,
    A magpie's spotted feathers lie
On the black earth spread white with rime,
The berries redden up to Christmas-time.
    What's Christmas-time without there be
    Some other in the house than we!

She sleeps up in the attic there
    Alone, poor maid. 'Tis but a stair
Betwixt us. Oh! my God! the down,
The soft young down of her, the brown,
The brown of her – her eyes, her hair, her hair!

In Nunhead Cemetery

It is the clay that makes the earth stick to his spade;
    He fills in holes like this year after year;
The others have gone; they were tired, and half afraid
    But I would rather be standing here;

There is nowhere else to go. I have seen this place
    From the windows of the train that's going past
Against the sky. This is rain on my face –
    It was raining here when I saw it last.

There is something horrible about a flower;
　This, broken in my hand, is one of those
He threw in just now: it will not live another hour;
　There are thousands more: you do not miss a rose.

One of the children hanging about
　Pointed at the whole dreadful heap and smiled
This morning, after THAT was carried out;
　There is something terrible about a child.

We were like children, last week, in the Strand;
　That was the day you laughed at me
Because I tried to make you understand
　The cheap, stale chap I used to be
　Before I saw the things you made me see.

This is not a real place; perhaps by-and-by
　I shall wake – I am getting drenched with all this rain:
To-morrow I will tell you about the eyes of the Crystal Palace
　　　　　　　　　　　　　　　　　　　　　train
　Looking down on us, and you will laugh and I shall see what
　　　　　　　　　　　　　　　　　　　you see again.

　Not here, not now. We said 'Not yet
　Across our low stone parapet
Will the quick shadows of the sparrows fall.'

　But still it was a lovely thing
　Through the grey months to wait for Spring
　With the birds that go a-gypsying
In the parks till the blue seas call.
　And next to these, you used to care
　For the lions in Trafalgar Square,
Who'll stand and speak for London when her bell of Judgment
　　　　　　　　　　　　　　　　　　　　　tolls –

And the gulls at Westminster that were
  The old sea-captain's souls.
To-day again the brown tide splashes, step by step, the river
                                                        stair,

  And the gulls are there!

By a month we have missed our Day:
  The children would have hung about
Round the carriage and over the way
  As you and I came out.

We should have stood on the gulls' black cliffs and heard the sea
  And seen the moon's white track,
I would have called, you would have come to me
  And kissed me back.

You have never done that: I do not know
  Why I stood staring at your bed
And heard you, though you spoke so low,
  But could not reach your hands, your little head.
There was nothing we could not do, you said,
  And you went, and I let you go!

Now I will burn you back, I will burn you through,
  Though I am damned for it we two will lie
  And burn, here where the starlings fly
  To these white stones from the wet sky – ;
  Dear, you will say this is not I –
It would not be you, it would not be you!

If for only a little while
   You will think of it you will understand,
     If you will touch my sleeve and smile
   As you did that morning in the Strand
     I can wait quietly with you
     Or go away if you want me to –
   God! What is God? but your face has gone and your hand!
     Let me stay here too.

     When I was quite a little lad
    At Christmas time we went half mad
     For joy of all the toys we had,
And then we used to sing about the sheep
     The shepherds watched by night;
We used to pray to Christ to keep
     Our small souls safe till morning light – ;
I am scared, I am staying with you to-night –
          Put me to sleep.

I shall stay here: here you can see the sky;
The houses in the streets are much too high;
   There is no one left to speak to there;
   Here they are everywhere,
And just above them fields and fields of roses lie –
If he would dig it all up again they would not die.

On the Road to the Sea

We passed each other, turned and stopped for half an hour, then
                              went our way,
  I who make other women smile did not make you –
But no man can move mountains in a day.
  So this hard thing is yet to do.

But first I want your life: – before I die I want to see
  The world that lies behind the strangeness of your eyes,
There is nothing gay or green there for my gathering, it may be,
      Yet on brown fields there lies
A haunting purple bloom: is there not something in grey skies
      And in grey sea?
  I want what world there is behind your eyes,
  I want your life and you will not give it me.

Now, if I look, I see you walking down the years,
Young, and through August fields – a face, a thought, a
                  swinging dream perched on a stile – ;
I would have liked (so vile we are!) to have taught you tears
      But most to have made you smile.

Today is not enough or yesterday: God sees it all –
Your length on sunny lawns, the wakeful rainy nights – ; tell
me – ; (how vain to ask), but it is not a question – just a call – ;
Show me then, only your notched inches climbing up the garden
                              wall,
      I like you best when you are small.

Is this a stupid thing to say
Not having spent with you one day?
No matter; I shall never touch your hair
Or hear the little tick behind your breast,
    Still it is there,
    And as a flying bird
Brushes the branches where it may not rest
    I have brushed your hand and heard
The child in you: I like that best

So small, so dark, so sweet; and were you also then too grave and
                                                                wise?
    Always I think. Then put your far off little hand in mine; – Oh!
                                                                let it rest;
I will not stare into the early world beyond the opening eyes,
    Or vex or scare what I love best.
    But I want your life before mine bleeds away –
        Here – not in heavenly hereafters – soon, –
        I want your smile this very afternoon,
    (The last of all my vices, pleasant people used to say,
        I wanted and I sometimes got – the Moon!)

    You know, at dusk, the last bird's cry,
    And round the house the flap of the bat's low flight,
        Trees that go black against the sky
    And then – how soon the night!

Now shadow of you on any bright road again,
And at the darkening end of this – what voice? Whose kiss? As if
                                                                you'd say!
It is not I who have walked with you, it will not be I who take
                                                                away
    Peace, peace, my little handful of the gleaner's grain
    From your reaped fields at the shut of day.

Peace! Would you not rather die
Reeling, – with all the cannons at your ear?
So, at least, would I,
And I may not be here
Tonight, tomorrow morning or next year.
Still I will let you keep your life a little while,
See dear?
I have made you smile.

MARY URSULA BETHELL

Response

When you wrote your letter it was April,
And you were glad that it was spring weather,
And that the sun shone out in turn with showers of rain.

I write in waning May and it is autumn,
And I am glad that my chrysanthemums
Are tied up fast to strong posts,
So that the south winds cannot beat them down.
I am glad that they are tawny coloured,
And fiery in the low west evening light.
And I am glad that one bush warbler
Still sings in the honey-scented wattle . . .

But oh, we have remembering hearts,
And we say 'How green it was in such and such an April,'
And 'Such and such an autumn was very golden,'
And 'Everything is for a very short time.'

Time

'Established' is a good word, much used in garden books,
'The plant, when established' . . .
Oh, become established quickly, quickly, garden!
For I am fugitive, I am very fugitive –

Those that come after me will gather these roses,
And watch, as I do now, the white wistaria
Burst, in the sunshine, from its pale green sheath.

Planned. Planted. Established. Then neglected,
Till at last the loiterer by the gate will wonder
At the old, old cottage, the old wooden cottage,
And say, 'One might build here, the view is glorious;
This must have been a pretty garden once.'

Warning of Winter

Give over, now, red roses;
Summer-long you told us,
Urgently unfolding, death-sweet, life-red,
Tidings of love. All's said. Give over.

Summer-long you placarded
Leafy shades with heart-red
Symbols. Who knew not love at first knows now,
Who had forgot has now remembered.

Let be, let be, lance-lilies,
Alert, pard-spotted, tilting
Poised anthers, flaming; have done flaming fierce;
Hard hearts were pierced long since, and stricken.

Give to the blast your thorn-crowns
Roses; and now be torn down
All you ardent lilies, your high-holden crests,
Havocked and cast to rest on the clammy ground.

Alas, alas, to darkness
Descends the flowered pathway,
To solitary places, deserts, utter night;
To issue in what hidden dawn of light hereafter?

But one, in dead of winter,
Divine *Agape*, kindles
Morning suns, new moons, lights starry trophies;
Says to the waste: Rejoice, and bring forth roses;
To the ice-fields: Let here spring thick bright lilies.

ANNA WICKHAM

The Fired Pot

In our town, people live in rows.
The only irregular thing in a street is the steeple;
And where that points to God only knows,
And not the poor disciplined people!

And I have watched the women growing old,
Passionate about pins, and pence, and soap,
Till the heart within my wedded breast grew cold,
And I lost hope.

But a young soldier came to our town,
He spoke his mind most candidly.
He asked me quickly to lie down,
And that was very good for me.

For though I gave him no embrace –
Remembering my duty –
He altered the expression of my face,
And gave me back my beauty.

Nervous Prostration

I married a man of the Croydon class
When I was twenty-two.
And I vex him, and he bores me
Till we don't know what to do!
It isn't good form in the Croydon class
To say you love your wife,
So I spend my days with the tradesmen's books
And pray for the end of life.

In green fields are blossoming trees
And a golden wealth of gorse,
And young birds sing for joy of worms:
It's perfectly clear, of course,
That it wouldn't be taste in the Croydon class
To sing over dinner or tea:
But I sometimes wish the gentleman
Would turn and talk to me!

But every man of the Croydon class
Lives in terror of joy and speech,
'Words are betrayers', 'Joys are brief'
The maxims their wise ones teach.
And for all my labour of love and life
I shall be clothed and fed,
And they'll give me an orderly funeral
When I'm still enough to be dead.

I married a man of the Croydon class
When I was twenty-two.
And I vex him, and he bores me
Till we don't know what to do!
And as I sit in his ordered house,
I feel I must sob or shriek,
To force a man of the Croydon class
To live, or to love, or to speak!

ELINOR WYLIE

Wild Peaches

1

When the world turns completely upside down
You say we'll emigrate to the Eastern Shore
Aboard a river-boat from Baltimore;
We'll live among wild peach trees, miles from town,
You'll wear a coonskin cap, and I a gown
Homespun, dyed butternut's dark gold color.
Lost, like your lotus-eating ancestor,
We'll swim in milk and honey till we drown.

The winter will be short, the summer long,
The autumn amber-hued, sunny and hot,
Tasting of cider and of scuppernong;
All seasons sweet, but autumn best of all.
The squirrels in their silver fur will fall
Like falling leaves, like fruit, before your shot.

2

The autumn frosts will lie upon the grass
Like bloom on grapes of purple-brown and gold.
The misted early mornings will be cold;
The little puddles will be roofed with glass.
The sun, which burns from copper into brass,
Melts these at noon, and makes the boys unfold
Their knitted mufflers; full as they can hold,
Fat pockets dribble chestnuts as they pass.

Peaches grow wild, and pigs can live in clover;
A barrel of salted herrings lasts a year;
The spring begins before the winter's over.
By February you may find the skins
Of garter snakes and water moccasins
Dwindled and harsh, dead-white and cloudy-clear.

3

When April pours the colors of a shell
Upon the hills, when every little creek
Is shot with silver from the Chesapeake
In shoals new-minted by the ocean swell,
When strawberries go begging, and the sleek
Blue plums lie open to the blackbird's beak,
We shall live well – we shall live very well.

The months between the cherries and the peaches
Are brimming cornucopias which spill
Fruits red and purple, somber-bloomed and black;
Then, down rich fields and frosty river beaches
We'll trample bright persimmons, while you kill
Bronze partridge, speckled quail, and canvasback.

4

Down to the Puritan marrow of my bones
There's something in this richness that I hate.
I love the look, austere, immaculate,
Of landscapes drawn in pearly monotones.
There's something in my very blood that owns
Bare hills, cold silver on a sky of slate,
A thread of water, churned to milky spate
Streaming through slanted pastures fenced with stones.

I love those skies, thin blue or snowy gray,
Those fields sparse-planted, rendering meager sheaves;
That spring, briefer than apple-blossom's breath,
Summer, so much too beautiful to stay,
Swift autumn, like a bonfire of leaves,
And sleepy winter, like the sleep of death.

Prophecy

I shall lie hidden in a hut
   In the middle of an alder wood,
With the back door blind and bolted shut,
   And the front door locked for good.

I shall lie folded like a saint,
   Lapped in a scented linen sheet,
On a bedstead striped with bright-blue paint,
   Narrow and cold and neat.

The midnight will be glassy black
   Behind the panes, with wind about
To set his mouth against a crack
   And blow the candle out.

FRANCES CORNFORD

To a Fat Lady Seen from the Train

Triolet

O why do you walk through the fields in gloves,
  Missing so much and so much?
O fat white woman whom nobody loves,
Why do you walk through the fields in gloves,
When the grass is soft as the breast of doves
  And shivering-sweet to the touch?
O why do you walk through the fields in gloves,
  Missing so much and so much?

A Recollection

My father's friend came once to tea.
He laughed and talked. He spoke to me.
But in another week they said
That friendly pink-faced man was dead.

'How sad . . .' they said, 'the best of men . . .
So I said too, 'How sad'; but then
Deep in my heart I thought, with pride,
'I know a person who has died'.

Childhood

I used to think that grown-up people chose
To have stiff backs and wrinkles round their nose,
And veins like small fat snakes on either hand,
On purpose to be grand.
Till through the banisters I watched one day
My great-aunt Etty's friend who was going away,
And how her onyx beads had come unstrung.
I saw her grope to find them as they rolled;
And then I knew that she was helplessly old,
As I was helplessly young.

Parting in Wartime

How long ago Hector took off his plume,
Not wanting that his little son should cry,
Then kissed his sad Andromache goodbye –
And now we three in Euston waiting-room.

H.D.

Helen

All Greece hates
the still eyes in the white face,
the lustre as of olives
where she stands,
and the white hands.

All Greece reviles
the wan face when she smiles,
hating it deeper still
when it grows wan and white,
remembering past enchantments
and past ills.

Greece sees unmoved,
God's daughter, born of love,
the beauty of cool feet
and slenderest knees,
could love indeed the maid,
only if she were laid,
white ash amid funereal cypresses.

Lethe

Nor skin nor hide nor fleece
    shall cover you,
nor curtain of crimson nor fine
shelter of cedar-wood be over you,
    nor the fir-tree
    nor the pine.

[35]

Nor sight of whin nor gorse
    nor river-yew,
nor fragrance of flowering bush,
nor wailing of reed-bird to waken you,
    nor of linnet,
    nor of thrush.

Nor word nor touch nor sight
    of lover, you
shall long through the night but for this:
the roll of the full tide to cover you
    without question,
    without kiss.

from Winter Love

5

So we were together
though I did not think of you
for ten years;

it is more than ten years
and the long time after;
I was with you in Calypso's cave?

no, no – I had never heard of her,
but I remember the curve of honey-flower
on an old wall, I recall

the honey-flower as I saw it
or seemed to see it
for the first time,

its horn was longer, whiter –
what do I mean?
'bite clear the stem

and suck the honey out,'
a child companion or old grandam
taught me to suck honey

from the honey-flower;
what is Calypso's cave?
that is your grotto, your adventure;

how could I love again, ever?
repetition, repetition, Achilles, Paris, Menelaus?
but you are right, you are right,

there is something left over,
the first unsatisfied desire –
the first time, that first kiss,

the rough stones of a wall,
the fragrance of honey-flowers, the bees,
and how I would have fallen but for a voice,

calling through the brambles
and tangle of bay-berry
and rough broom,

Helen, Helen, come home;
there was a Helen before there was a War,
but who remembers her?

from Sigil

XI

If you take the moon in your hands
and turn it round
(heavy, slightly tarnished platter)
you're there;

if you pull dry seaweed from the sand
and turn it round
and wonder at the underside's bright amber,
your eyes

look out as they did here,
(you don't remember)
when my soul turned round,

perceiving the other-side of everything,
mullein-leaf, dog-wood leaf, moth-wing
and dandelion-seed under the ground.

ELIZABETH DARYUSH

Still-Life

Through the open french window the warm sun
lights up the polished breakfast-table, laid
round a bowl of crimson roses, for one –
a service of Worcester porcelain, arrayed
near it a melon, peaches, figs, small hot
rolls in a napkin, fairy rack of toast,
butter in ice, high silver coffee pot,
and, heaped on a salver, the morning's post.

She comes over the lawn, the young heiress,
from her early walk in her garden-wood
feeling that life's a table set to bless
her delicate desires with all that's good,

that even the unopened future lies
like a love-letter, full of sweet surprise.

MARIANNE MOORE

I May, I might, I must

If you will tell me why the fen
appears impassable, I then
will tell you why I think that I
can get across it if I try.

The Steeple-Jack

Revised, 1961

Dürer would have seen a reason for living
   in a town like this, with eight stranded whales
to look at; with the sweet sea air coming into your house
on a fine day, from water etched
   with waves as formal as the scales
on a fish.

One by one in two's and three's, the seagulls keep
   flying back and forth over the town clock,
or sailing around the lighthouse without moving their wings –
rising steadily with a slight
   quiver of the body – or flock
mewing where

a sea the purple of the peacock's neck is
   paled to greenish azure as Dürer changed
the pine green of the Tyrol to peacock blue and guinea
gray. You can see a twenty-five-
   pound lobster; and fish nets arranged
to dry. The

whirlwind fife-and-drum of the storm bends the salt
   marsh grass, disturbs stars in the sky and the
star on the steeple; it is a privilege to see so
much confusion. Disguised by what
   might seem the opposite, the sea-
side flowers and

trees are favored by the fog so that you have
   the tropics at first hand: the trumpet vine,
foxglove, giant snapdragon, a salpiglossis that has
spots and stripes; morning-glories, gourds,
   or moon-vines trained on fishing twine
at the back door:

cattails, flags, blueberries and spiderwort,
   striped grass, lichens, sunflowers, asters, daisies –
yellow and crab-claw ragged sailors with green bracts – toad-
                                     plant,
petunias, ferns; pink lilies, blue
   ones, tigers; poppies; black sweet-peas.
The climate

is not right for the banyan, frangipani, or
   jack-fruit trees; or for exotic serpent
life. Ring lizard and snakeskin for the foot, if you see fit;
but here they've cats, not cobras, to
   keep down the rats. The diffident
little newt

with white pin-dots on black horizontal spaced-
   out bands lives here; yet there is nothing that
ambition can buy or take away. The college student
named Ambrose sits on the hillside
   with his not-native books and hat
and sees boats

at sea progress white and rigid as if in
   a groove. Liking an elegance of which
the source is not bravado, he knows by heart the antique
sugar-bowl shaped summerhouse of
   interlacing slats, and the pitch
of the church

spire, not true, from which a man in scarlet lets
   down a rope as a spider spins a thread;
he might be part of a novel, but on the sidewalk a
sign says C. J. Poole, Steeple-Jack,
   in black and white; and one in red
and white says

Danger. The church portico has four fluted
   columns, each a single piece of stone, made
modester by whitewash. This would be a fit haven for
waifs, children, animals, prisoners,
   and presidents who have repaid
sin-driven

senators by not thinking about them. The
   place has a schoolhouse, a post-office in a
store, fish-houses, hen-houses, a three-masted
   schooner on
the stocks. The hero, the student,
   the steeple-jack, each in his way,
is at home.

It could not be dangerous to be living
   in a town like this, of simple people,
who have a steeple-jack placing danger signs by the church
while he is gilding the solid-
   pointed star, which on a steeple
stands for hope.

The Jerboa

TOO MUCH

A Roman had an
artist, a freedman,
   contrive a cone – pine cone
   or fir cone – with holes for a fountain. Placed on
     the Prison of St Angelo, this cone
     of the Pompeys which is known

now as the Popes', passed
for art. A huge cast
   bronze, dwarfing the peacock
   statue in the garden of the Vatican,
     it looks like a work of art made to give
     to a Pompey, or native

of Thebes. Others could
build, and understood
   making colossi and
   how to use slaves, and kept crocodiles and put
     baboons on the necks of giraffes to pick
     fruit, and used serpent magic.

They had their men tie
hippopotami
   and bring out dappled dog-
   cats to course antelopes, dikdik, and ibex;
     or used small eagles. They looked on as theirs,
     impalas and onigers,

the wild ostrich herd
with hard feet and bird
  necks rearing back in the
    dust like a serpent preparing to strike, cranes,
      mongooses, storks, anoas, Nile geese;
      and there were gardens for these –

combining planes, dates,
limes, and pomegranates,
  in avenues – with square
    pools of pink flowers, tame fish, and small frogs. Besides
      yarns dyed with indigo, and red cotton,
      they had a flax which they spun

into fine linen
cordage for yachtsmen.
  These people liked small things;
    they gave to boys little paired playthings such as
      nests of eggs, ichneumon and snake, paddle
      and raft, badger and camel;

and made toys for them-
selves: the royal totem;
  and toilet boxes marked
    with the contents. Lords and ladies put goose-grease
      paint in round bone boxes – the pivoting
      lid incised with a duck-wing

or reverted duck-
head; kept in a buck
  or rhinoceros horn,
    the ground horn; and locust oil in stone locusts.
      It was a picture with a fine distance;
      of drought, and of assistance

in time, from the Nile
rising slowly, while
   the pig-tailed monkey on
   slab hands, with arched-up slack-slung gait, and the brown
     dandy looked at the jasmine two-leafed twig
     and bud, cactus pads, and fig.

Dwarfs here and there, lent
to an evident
   poetry of frog grays,
   duck-egg greens, and eggplant blues, a fantasy
     and a verisimilitude that were
     right to those with, everywhere,

power over the poor.
The bees' food is your
   food. Those who tended flower-
   beds and stables were like the king's cane in the
     form of a hand, or the folding bedroom
     made for his mother of whom

he was fond. Princes
clad in queens' dresses,
   calla or petunia
   white, that trembled at the edge, and queens in a
     king's underskirt of fine-twilled thread like silk-
     worm gut, as bee-man and milk-

maid, kept divine cows
and bees; limestone brows,
   and gold-foil wings. They made
   basalt serpents and portraits of beetles; the
     king gave his name to them and he was named
     for them. He feared snakes, and tamed

Pharaoh's rat, the rust-
backed mongoose. No bust
  of it was made, but there
    was pleasure for the rat. Its restlessness was
      its excellence; it was praised for its wit;
      and the jerboa, like it,

a small desert rat,
and not famous, that
  lives without water, has
    happiness. Abroad seeking food, or at home
      in its burrow, the Sahara fieldmouse
      has a shining silver house

of sand. O rest and
joy, the boundless sand,
  the stupendous sandspout,
    no water, no palm trees, no ivory bed,
      tiny cactus; but one would not be he
      who has nothing but plenty.

ABUNDANCE

Africanus meant
the conqueror sent
  from Rome. It should mean the
    untouched: the sand-brown jumping-rat – free-born; and
      the blacks, that choice race with an elegance
      ignored by one's ignorance.

Part terrestrial,
and part celestial,
  Jacob saw, cudgel staff
    in claw hand – steps of air and air angels; his
      friends were the stones. The translucent mistake
      of the desert, does not make

hardship for one who
can rest and then do
   the opposite – launching
   as if on wings, from its match-thin hind legs, in
      daytime or at night; with the tail as a weight,
      undulated out by speed, straight.

Looked at by daylight,
the underside's white,
   though the fur on the back
   is buff-brown like the breast of the fawn-breasted
      bower-bird. It hops like the fawn-breast, but has
      chipmunk contours – perceived as

it turns its bird head –
the nap directed
   neatly back and blending
   with the ear which reiterates the slimness
      of the body. The fine hairs on the tail,
      repeating the other pale

markings, lengthen until
at the tip they fill
   out in a tuft – black and
   white; strange detail of the simplified creature,
      fish-shaped and silvered to steel by the force
      of the large desert moon. Course

the jerboa, or
plunder its food store,
   and you will be cursed. It
   honors the sand by assuming its color;
      closed upper paws seeming one with the fur
      in its flight from a danger.

By fifths and sevenths,
in leaps of two lengths,
  like the uneven notes
  of the Bedouin flute, it stops its gleaning
    on little wheel castors, and makes fern-seed
    footprints with kangaroo speed.

Its leaps should be set
to the flageolet;
  pillar body erect
  on a three-cornered smooth-working Chippendale
    claw – propped on hind legs, and tail as third toe,
    between leaps to its burrow.

The Fish

  wade
  through black jade.
    Of the crow-blue mussel shells, one keeps
    adjusting the ash heaps;
      opening and shutting itself like

  an
  injured fan.
    The barnacles which encrust the side
    of the wave, cannot hide
      there for the submerged shafts of the

  sun,
  split like spun
    glass, move themselves with spotlight swiftness
    into the crevices –
      in and out, illuminating

the
turquoise sea
   of bodies. The water drives a wedge
   of iron through the iron edge
     of the cliff; whereupon the stars,

pink
rice-grains, ink-
   bespattered jellyfish, crabs like green
   lilies, and submarine
     toadstools, slide each on the other.

All
external
   marks of abuse are present on this
   defiant edifice –
     all the physical features of

ac-
cident – lack
   of cornice, dynamite grooves, burns, and
   hatchet strokes, these things stand
     out on it; the chasm side is

dead.
Repeated
   evidence has proved that it can live
   on what can not revive
     its youth. The sea grows old in it.

Poetry

Original version

I, too, dislike it: there are things that are important beyond all this
fiddle.
  Reading it, however, with a perfect contempt for it, one
discovers in
  it after all, a place for the genuine.
    Hands that can grasp, eyes
    that can dilate, hair that can rise
      if it must, these things are important not because a

high-sounding interpretation can be put upon them but because
they are
  useful. When they become so derivative as to become
unintelligible,
  the same thing may be said for all of us, that we
    do not admire what
    we cannot understand: the bat
      holding on upside down or in quest of something to

eat, elephants pushing, a wild horse taking a roll, a tireless wolf
under
  a tree, the immovable critic twitching his skin like a horse that
feels a flea, the base-
  ball fan, the statistician
    nor is it valid
      to discriminate against 'business documents and

school-books'; all these phenomena are important. One must
                              make a distinction
   however: when dragged into prominence by half poets, the
                              result is not poetry,
      nor till the poets among us can be
      'literalists of
      the imagination' – above
         insolence and triviality and can present

for inspection, 'imaginary gardens with real toads in them,' shall
                              we have
   it. In the meantime, if you demand on the one hand,
   the raw material of poetry in
      all its rawness and
      that which is on the other hand
         genuine, you are interested in poetry.

Critics and Connoisseurs

There is a great amount of poetry in unconscious
   fastidiousness. Certain Ming
      products, imperial floor coverings of coach-
   wheel yellow, are well enough in their way but I have seen
                              something

      that I like better – a
         mere childish attempt to make an imperfectly bal-
         lasted animal stand up,
         similar determination to make a pup
            eat his meat from the plate.

I remember a swan under the willows in Oxford,
  with flamingo-colored, maple-
    leaflike feet. It reconnoitered like a battle-
  ship. Disbelief and conscious fastidiousness were
     ingredients in its
       disinclination to move. Finally its hardihood was
         not proof against its
       proclivity to more fully appraise such bits
       of food as the stream

bore counter to it; it made away with what I gave it
  to eat. I have seen this swan and
   I have seen you; I have seen ambition without
  understanding in a variety of forms. Happening to stand
    by an ant-hill, I have
       seen a fastidious ant carrying a stick north, south,
         east, west, till it turned on
       itself, struck out from the flower bed into the lawn,
       and returned to the point

from which it had started. Then abandoning the stick as
  useless and overtaxing its
   jaws with a particle of whitewash – pill-like but
  heavy – it again went through the same course of procedure.
       What is
     there in being able
       to say that one has dominated the stream in an attitude
                 of self-defense;
       in proving that one has had the experience
       of carrying a stick?

England

with its baby rivers and little towns, each with its abbey or its
cathedral,
with voices – one voice perhaps, echoing through the transept –
the
criterion of suitability and convenience: and Italy
with its equal shores – contriving an epicureanism
from which the grossness has been extracted,

and Greece with its goat and its gourds,
the nest of modified illusions: and France,
the 'chrysalis of the nocturnal butterfly',
in whose products mystery of construction
diverts one from what was originally one's object –
substance at the core: and the East with its snails, its emotional

shorthand and jade cockroaches, its rock crystal and its
imperturbability,
all of museum quality: and America where there
is the little old ramshackle victoria in the south,
where cigars are smoked on the street in the north:
where there are no proofreaders, no silkworms, no digressions;

the wild man's land: grassless, linksless, languageless country in
which letters are written
not in Spanish, not in Greek, not in Latin, not in shorthand,
but in plain American which cats and dogs can read!
The letter *a* in psalm and calm when
pronounced with the sound of *a* in candle, is very noticeable, but

why should continents of misapprehension
have to be accounted for by the fact?
Does it follow that because there are poisonous toadstools
which resemble mushrooms, both are dangerous?
Of mettlesomeness which may be mistaken for appetite,
of heat which may appear to be haste,
no conclusions may be drawn.

To have misapprehended the matter is to have confessed that one
                                   has not looked far enough.
The sublimated wisdom of China, Egyptian discernment,
the cataclysmic torrent of emotion
compressed in the verbs of the Hebrew language,
the books of the man who is able to say,
'I envy nobody but him, and him only,
who catches more fish than
I do' – the flower and fruit of all that noted superiority –
if not stumbled upon in America,
must one imagine that it is not there?
It has never been confined to one locality.

A Grave

Man looking into the sea,
taking the view from those who have as much right to it as you
                                   have to it yourself,
it is human nature to stand in the middle of a thing,
but you cannot stand in the middle of this;
the sea has nothing to give but a well excavated grave.
The firs stand in a procession, each with an emerald turkey foot at
                                   the top,
reserved as their contours, saying nothing;
repression, however, is not the most obvious characteristic of the
                                   sea;
the sea is a collector, quick to return a rapacious look.

[54]

There are others besides you who have worn that look –
whose expression is no longer a protest; the fish no longer
                                        investigate them
for their bones have not lasted:
men lower nets, unconscious of the fact that they are desecrating
                                        a grave,
and row quickly away – the blades of the oars
moving together like the feet of water spiders as if there were no
                                        such thing as death.
The wrinkles progress among themselves in a phalanx – beautiful
                                        under networks of foam,
and fade breathlessly while the sea rustles in and out of the
                                        seaweed;
the birds swim through the air at top speed, emitting catcalls as
                                        heretofore –
the tortoise shell scourges about the feet of the cliffs, in motion
                                        beneath them;
and the ocean, under the pulsation of lighthouses and noise of
                                        bell buoys,
advances as usual, looking as if it were not that ocean in which
                                        dropped things are bound to sink –
in which if they turn and twist, it is neither with volition nor
                                        consciousness.

To a Snail

If 'compression is the first grace of style',
you have it. Contractility is a virtue
as modesty is a virtue.
It is not the acquisition of any one thing
that is able to adorn,
or the incidental quality that occurs
as a concomitant of something well said,
that we value in style,
but the principle that is hid:
in the absence of feet, 'a method of conclusions';
'a knowledge of principles',
in the curious phenomenon of your occipital horn.

Silence

My father used to say,
'Superior people never make long visits,
have to be shown Longfellow's grave
or the glass flowers at Harvard.
Self-reliant like the cat –
that takes its prey to privacy,
the mouse's limp tail hanging like a shoelace from its mouth –
they sometimes enjoy solitude,
and can be robbed of speech
by speech which has delighted them.
The deepest feeling always shows itself in silence;
not in silence, but restraint.'
Nor was he insincere in saying, 'Make my house your inn.'
Inns are not residences.

Spenser's Ireland

has not altered; –
  a place as kind as it is green,
  the greenest place I've never seen.
Every name is a tune.
Denunciations do not affect
    the culprit; nor blows, but it
is torture to him to not be spoken to.
They're natural –
     the coat, like Venus'
mantle lined with stars,
buttoned close at the neck – the sleeves new from disuse.

If in Ireland
  they play the harp backward at need,
  and gather at midday the seed
of the fern, eluding
their 'giants all covered with iron', might
    there be fern seed for unlearn-
ing obduracy and for reinstating
the enchantment?
     Hindered characters
seldom have mothers
in Irish stories, but they all have grandmothers.

It was Irish;
  a match not a marriage was made
  when my great great grandmother'd said
with native genius for
disunion, 'Although your suitor be
    perfection, one objection
is enough; he is not
Irish.' Outwitting
     the fairies, befriending the furies,

whoever again
and again says, 'I'll never give in', never sees

that you're not free
  until you've been made captive by
  supreme belief – credulity
you say? When large dainty
fingers tremblingly divide the wings
    of the fly for mid-July
with a needle and wrap it with peacock tail,
or tie wool and
      buzzard's wing, their pride,
like the enchanter's
is in care, not madness. Concurring hands divide

flax for damask
  that when bleached by Irish weather
  has the silvered chamois-leather
water-tightness of a
skin. Twisted torcs and gold new-moon-shaped
    lunulae aren't jewelry
like the purple-coral fuchsia-tree's. Eire –
the guillemot
      so neat and the hen
of the heath and the
linnet spinet-sweet – bespeak relentlessness? Then

they are to me
  like enchanted Earl Gerald who
  changed himself into a stag, to
a great green-eyed cat of
the mountain. Discommodity makes
    them invisible; they've dis-
appeared. The Irish say your trouble is their

trouble and your
joy their joy? I wish
I could believe it;
I am troubled, I'm dissatisfied, I'm Irish.

The Pangolin

Another armored animal – scale
lapping scale with spruce-cone regularity until they
form the uninterrupted central
tail-row! This near artichoke with head and legs and grit-
equipped gizzard,
the night miniature artist engineer is,
yes, Leonardo da Vinci's replica –
impressive animal and toiler of whom we seldom hear.
Armor seems extra. But for him,
the closing ear-ridge –
or bare ear lacking even this small
eminence and similarly safe

contracting nose and eye apertures
impenetrably closable, are not; a true ant-eater,
not cockroach-eater, who endures
exhausting solitary trips through unfamiliar ground at night,
returning before sunrise; stepping in the moonlight,
on the moonlight peculiarly, that the outside
edges of his hands may bear the weight and save the
claws
for digging. Serpentined about
the tree, he draws
away from danger unpugnaciously,
with no sound but a harmless hiss; keeping

the fragile grace of the Thomas-
    of-Leighton Buzzard Westminster Abbey wrought-iron vine,
                                                  or

rolls himself into a ball that has
   power to defy all effort to unroll it; strongly intailed, neat
  head for core, and neck not breaking off, with curled-in feet.
      Nevertheless he has sting-proof scales; and nest
        of rocks closed with earth from inside, which he can
                                thus darken.
      Sun and moon and day and night and man and beast
       each with a splendor
         which man in all his vileness cannot
         set aside; each with an excellence!

'Fearful yet to be feared', the armored
   ant-eater met by the driver-ant does not turn back, but
engulfs what he can, the flattened sword-
  edged leafpoints on the tail and artichoke set leg- and body-
                                  plates
  quivering violently when it retaliates
    and swarms on him. Compact like the furled fringed frill
     on-the hat-brim of Gargallo's hollow iron head of a
    matador, he will drop and will
      then walk away
        unhurt, although if unintruded on,
        he cautiously works down the tree, helped

by his tail. The giant-pangolin-
    tail, graceful tool, as prop or hand or broom or ax, tipped like
an elephant's trunk with special skin,
  is not lost on this ant- and stone-swallowing uninjurable
  artichoke which simpletons thought a living fable
      whom the stones had nourished, whereas ants had done
        so. Pangolins are not aggressive animals; between
      dusk and day they have the not unchain-like machine-like
        form and frictionless creep of a thing
        made graceful by adversities, con-

versities. To explain grace requires
  a curious hand. If that which is at all were not forever,
why would those who graced the spires
  with animals and gathered there to rest, on cold luxurious
  low stone seats – a monk and monk and monk – between the
                                thus
      ingenious roof supports, have slaved to confuse
        grace with a kindly manner, time in which to pay a debt,
      the cure for sins, a graceful use
      of what are yet
        approved stone mullions branching out across
        the perpendiculars? A sailboat

was the first machine. Pangolins, made
  for moving quietly also, are models of exactness,
on four legs; on hind feet plantigrade,
  with certain postures of a man. Beneath sun and moon, man
                              slaving
  to make his life more sweet, leaves half the flowers worth
                            having,
      needing to choose wisely how to use his strength;
        a paper-maker like the wasp; a tractor of foodstuffs,
      like the ant; spidering a length
      of web from bluffs
        above a stream; in fighting, mechanicked
        like the pangolin; capsized in

[61]

disheartenment. Bedizened or stark
    naked, man, the self, the being we call human, writing-
master to this world, griffons a dark
   'Like does not like like that is obnoxious'; and writes error with
                                 four

  r's. Among animals, *one* has a sense of humor.
      Humor saves a few steps, it saves years. Unignorant,
        modest and unemotional, and all emotion,
      he has everlasting vigor,
        power to grow,
          though there are few creatures who can make one
          breathe faster and make one erecter.

Not afraid of anything is he,
    and then goes cowering forth, tread paced to meet an
                               obstacle
at every step. Consistent with the
  formula – warm blood, no gills, two pairs of hands and a few
                           hairs – that
  is a mammal; there he sits in his own habitat,
      serge-clad, strong-shod. The prey of fear, he, always
        curtailed, extinguished, thwarted by the dusk, work
                           partly done,
      says to the alternating blaze,
       'Again the sun!
         anew each day; and new and new and new,
         that comes into and steadies my soul.'

The Paper Nautilus

For authorities whose hopes
are shaped by mercenaries?
    Writers entrapped by
    teatime fame and by
commuters' comforts? Not for these
    the paper nautilus
    constructs her thin glass shell.

Giving her perishable
souvenir of hope, a dull
    white outside and smooth-
    edged inner surface
glossy as the sea, the watchful
    maker of it guards it
    day and night; she scarcely

eats until the eggs are hatched.
Buried eightfold in her eight
    arms, for she is in
    a sense a devil-
fish, her glass ram's-horn-cradled freight
    is hid but is not crushed;
    as Hercules, bitten

by a crab loyal to the hydra,
was hindered to succeed,
    the intensively
    watched eggs coming from
the shell free it when they are freed –
    leaving its wasp-nest flaws
    of white on white, and close-

laid Ionic chiton-folds
like the lines in the mane of
a Parthenon horse,
round which the arms had
wound themselves as if they knew love
is the only fortress
strong enough to trust to.

EDITH SITWELL

Sir Beelzebub

When
Sir
Beelzebub called for his syllabub in the hotel in Hell
      Where Proserpine first fell,
Blue as the gendarmerie were the waves of the sea,
      (Rocking and shocking the bar-maid).

Nobody comes to give him his rum but the
Rim of the sky hippopotamus-glum
Enhances the chances to bless with a benison
Alfred Lord Tennyson crossing the bar laid
With cold vegetation from pale deputations
Of temperance workers (all signed In Memoriam)
Hoping with glory to trip up the Laureate's feet,
      (Moving in classical metres) . . .

Like Balaclava, the lava came down from the
Roof, and the sea's blue wooden gendarmerie
Took them in charge while Beelzebub roared for his rum.
    . . . None of them come!

EDNA ST VINCENT MILLAY

Childhood Is the Kingdom Where Nobody Dies

Childhood is not from birth to a certain age and at a certain age
The child is grown, and puts away childish things.
Childhood is the kingdom where nobody dies.

Nobody that matters, that is. Distant relatives of course
Die, whom one never has seen or has seen for an hour,
And they gave one candy in a pink-and-green striped bag, or
    a jack-knife,
And went away, and cannot really be said to have lived at all.

And cats die. They lie on the floor and lash their tails,
And their reticent fur is suddenly all in motion
With fleas that one never knew were there,
Polished and brown, knowing all there is to know,
Trekking off into the living world.
You fetch a shoe-box, but it's much too small, because she won't
    curl up now:
So you find a bigger box, and bury her in the yard, and weep.

But you do not wake up a month from then, two months,
A year from then, two years, in the middle of the night
And weep, with your knuckles in your mouth, and say Oh, God!
    Oh, God!
Childhood is the kingdom where nobody dies that matters, –
    mothers and fathers don't die.

And if you have said, 'For heaven's sake, must you always be
    kissing a person?'
Or, 'I do wish to gracious you'd stop tapping on the window
    with your thimble!'
Tomorrow, or even the day after tomorrow if you're busy having
    fun,
Is plenty of time to say, 'I'm sorry, mother.'

To be grown up is to sit at the table with people who have died,
    who neither listen nor speak;
Who do not drink their tea, though they always said
Tea was such a comfort.

Run down into the cellar and bring up the last jar of raspberries;
    they are not tempted.
Flatter them, ask them what it was they said exactly
That time, to the bishop, or to the overseer, or to Mrs Mason;
They are not taken in.
Shout at them, get red in the face, rise,
Drag them up out of their chairs by their stiff shoulders and
    shake them and yell at them;
They are not startled; they are not even embarrassed; they slide
    back into their chairs.

Your tea is cold now.
You drink it standing up,
And leave the house.

First Fig

My candle burns at both ends;
    It will not last the night;
But ah, my foes, and oh, my friends –
    It gives a lovely light!

Passer Mortuus Est

Death devours all lovely things:
    Lesbia with her sparrow
Shares the darkness, – presently
    Every bed is narrow.

Unremembered as old rain
    Dries the sheer libation;
And the little petulant hand
    Is an annotation.

After all, my erstwhile dear,
    My no longer cherished,
Need we say it was not love,
    Just because it perished?

The Strawberry Shrub

Strawberry Shrub, old-fashioned, quaint as quinces,
Hard to find in a world where neon and noise
Have flattened the ends of the three more subtle senses;
And blare and magenta are all that a child enjoys.

More brown than red the bloom – it is a dense color;
Color of dried blood; color of the key of F.
Tie it in your handkerchief, Dorcas, take it to school
To smell. But no, as I said, it is browner than red; it is duller
Than history, tinnier than algebra; and you are color-deaf.

Purple, a little, the bloom, like musty chocolate;
Purpler than the purple avens of the wet fields;
But brown and red and hard and hiding its fragrance;
More like an herb it is: it is not exuberant.
You must bruise it a bit: it does not exude; it yields.

Clinker-built, the bloom, over-lapped its petals
Like clapboards; like a boat I had; like the feathers of a wing;
Not graceful, not at all Grecian, something from the provinces;
A chunky, ruddy, beautiful Boeotian thing.

Take it to school, knotted in your handkerchief, Dorcas,
Corner of your handkerchief, take it to school, and see
What your teacher says; show your pretty teacher the curious
Strawberry Shrub you took to school for me.

Sonnet xxix

Pity me not because the light of day
At close of day no longer walks the sky;
Pity me not for beauties passed away
From field and thicket as the year goes by;
Pity me not the waning of the moon,
Nor that the ebbing tide goes out to sea,
Nor that a man's desire is hushed so soon,
And you no longer look with love on me.
This have I known always: Love is no more
Than the wide blossom which the wind assails,
Than the great tide that treads the shifting shore,
Strewing fresh wreckage gathered in the gales:
Pity me that the heart is slow to learn
What the swift mind beholds at every turn.

SYLVIA TOWNSEND WARNER

'Now in this long-deferred spring . . .

Now in this long-
deferred spring,
Blackthorn bush by the way-
side what do you say?

Summer was a burning fever,
Winter a cold fever.
I was spared by neither.

But yet your cramped boughs
are pricked with flowers.

By rote, by rote,
These blossoms I put out.
They have not anything
to do with this spring.

They are but the badge
of an old pledge.
Farewell, and overlook
these white ashes among the black.

King Duffus

When all the witches were haled to the stake and burned;
When their least ashes were swept up and drowned,
King Duffus opened his eyes and looked round.

For half a year they had trussed him in their spell:
Parching, scorching, roaring, he was blackened as a coal.
Now he wept like a freshet in April.

Tears ran like quicksilver through his rocky beard.
Why have you wakened me, he said, with a clattering sword?
Why have you snatched me back from the green yard?

There I sat feasting under the cool linden shade;
The beer in the silver cup was ever renewed,
I was at peace there, I was well-bestowed:

My crown lay lightly on my brow as a clot of foam,
My wide mantle was yellow as the flower of the broom,
Hale and holy I was in mind and in limb.

I sat among poets and among philosophers,
Carving fat bacon for the mother of Christ;
Sometimes we sang, sometimes we conversed.

Why did you summon me back from the midst of that meal
To a vexed kingdom and a smoky hall?
Could I not stay at least until dewfall?

Gloriana Dying

None shall gainsay me. I will lie on the floor.
Hitherto from horseback, throne, balcony,
I have looked down upon your looking up.
Those sands are run. Now I reverse the glass
And bid henceforth your homage downward, falling
Obedient and unheeded as leaves in autumn
To quilt the wakeful study I must make
Examining my kingdom from below.
How tall my people are! Like a race of trees

[71]

They sway, sigh, nod heads, rustle above me,
And their attentive eyes are distant as starshine.
I have still cherished the handsome and well-made:
No queen has better masts within her forests
Growing, nor prouder and more restive minds
Scabbarded in the loyalty of subjects;
No virgin has had better worship than I.
No, no! Leave me alone, woman! I will not
Be put into a bed. Do you suppose
That I who've ridden through all weathers, danced
Under a treasury's weight of jewels, sat
Myself to stone through sermons and addresses,
Shall come to harm by sleeping on a floor?
Not that I sleep. A bed were good enough
If that were in my mind. But I am here
For a deep study and contemplation,
And as Persephone, and the red vixen,
Go underground to sharpen their wits,
I have left my dais to learn a new policy
Through watching of your feet, and as the Indian
Lays all his listening body along the earth
I lie in wait for the reverberation
Of things to come and dangers threatening.
Is that the Bishop praying? Let him pray on.
If his knees tire his faith can cushion them.
How the poor man grieves Heaven with news of me!
Deposuit superbos. But no hand
Other than my own has put me down –
Not feebleness enforced on brain or limb,
Not fear, misgiving, fantasy, age, palsy,
Has felled me. I lie here by my own will,
And by the curiosity of a queen.
I dare say there is not in all England
One who lies closer to the ground than I.
Not the traitor in the condemned hold
Whose few straws edge away from under his weight

Of ironed fatality; not the shepherd
Huddled for cold under the hawthorn bush,
Nor the long, dreaming country lad who lies
Scorching his book before the dying brand.

LOUISE BOGAN

The Frightened Man

In fear of the rich mouth
I kissed the thin, –
Even that was a trap
To snare me in.

Even she, so long
The frail, the scentless,
Is become strong
And proves relentless.

O, forget her praise,
And how I sought her
Through a hazardous maze
By shafted water.

The Crows

The woman who has grown old
And knows desire must die,
Yet turns to love again,
Hears the crows' cry.

She is a stem long hardened,
A weed that no scythe mows.
The heart's laughter will be to her
The crying of the crows,

Who slide in the air with the same voice
Over what yields not, and what yields,
Alike in spring, and when there is only bitter
Winter-burning in the fields.

Last Hill in a Vista

Come, let us tell the weeds in ditches
How we are poor, who once had riches,
And lie out in the sparse and sodden
Pastures that the cows have trodden,
The while an autumn night seals down
The comforts of the wooden town.

Come, let us counsel some cold stranger
How we sought safety, but loved danger.
So, with stiff walls about us, we
Chose this more fragile boundary:
Hills, where light poplars, the firm oak,
Loosen into a little smoke.

Evening in the Sanitarium

The free evening fades, outside the windows fastened with
decorative iron grilles.
The lamps are lighted; the shades drawn; the nurses are watching
a little.
It is the hour of the complicated knitting on the safe bone needles;
of the games of anagrams and bridge;
The deadly game of chess; the book held up like a mask.

The period of the wildest weeping, the fiercest delusion, is over.
The women rest their tired half-healed hearts; they are almost
well.
Some of them will stay almost well always: the blunt-faced
woman whose thinking dissolved
Under academic discipline; the manic-depressive girl
Now leveling off; one paranoiac afflicted with jealousy.
Another with persecution. Some alleviation has been possible.

O fortunate bride, who never again will become elated after
childbirth!
O lucky older wife, who has been cured of feeling unwanted!
To the surburban railway station you will return, return,
To meet forever Jim home on the 5:35.
You will be again as normal and selfish and heartless as anybody
else.

There is life left: the piano says it with its octave smile.
The soft carpets pad the thump and splinter of the suicide to be.
Everything will be splendid: the grandmother will not drink
habitually.
The fruit salad will bloom on the plate like a bouquet
And the garden produce the blue-ribbon aquilegia.
The cats will be glad; the fathers feel justified; the mothers
relieved.
The sons and husbands will no longer need to pay the bills.
Childhoods will be put away, the obscene nightmare abated.

At the ends of the corridors the baths are running.
Mrs C. again feels the shadow of the obsessive idea.
Miss R. looks at the mantelpiece, which must mean something.

RUTH PITTER

The Sparrow's Skull

Memento Mori. Written at the Fall of France.

The kingdoms fall in sequence, like the waves on the shore.
All save divine and desperate hopes go down, they are no more.
Solitary is our place, the castle in the sea,
And I muse on those I have loved, and on those who have loved
me.

I gather up my loves, and keep them all warm,
While above our heads blows the bitter storm:
The blessed natural loves, of life-supporting flame,
And those whose name is Wonder, which have no other name.

The skull is in my hand, the minute cup of bone,
And I remember her, the tame, the loving one,
Who came in at the window, and seemed to have a mind
More towards sorrowful man than to those of her own kind.

She came for a long time, but at length she grew old;
And on her death-day she came, so feeble and so bold;
And all day, as if knowing what the day would bring,
She waited by the window, with her head beneath her wing.

And I will keep the skull, for in the hollow here
Lodged the minute brain that had outgrown a fear;
Transcended an old terror, and found a new love,
And entered a strange life, a world it was not of.

Even so, dread God! even so, my Lord!
The fire is at my feet, and at my breast the sword:
And I must gather up my soul, and clap my wings, and flee
Into the heart of terror, to find myself in thee.

[77]

Morning Glory

With a pure colour there is little one can do:
Of a pure thing there is little one can say.
We are dumb in the face of that cold blush of blue,
Called glory, and enigmatic as the face of day.

A couple of optical tricks are there for the mind;
See how the azure darkens as we recede:
Like the delectable mountains left behind,
Region and colour too absolute for our need.

Or putting an eye too close, until it blurs,
You see a firmament, a ring of sky,
With a white radiance in it, a universe,
And something there that might seem to sing and fly.

Only the double sex, the usual thing;
But it calls to mind spirit, it seems like one
Who hovers in brightness suspended and shimmering,
Crying Holy and hanging in the eye of the sun.

And there is one thing more; as in despair
The eye dwells on that ribbed pentagonal round,
A cold sidereal whisper brushes the ear,
A prescient tingling, a prophecy of sound.

FRANCES BELLERBY

A Clear Shell

Then fire burned my body to a clear shell.
Though whether the fanning tempest blew from hell
Or heaven I could not, cannot, tell –
Who have no sense
Left for so nice a difference.

But I learned the essential function of extreme pain –
Of liquid fire pouring again and again
And again through the horrified body: such pain
Makes wholly innocent.
Therefore am I impenitent

Today. Today ask no forgiveness,
Having nothing to be forgiven. And my soul, no less
House-proud than at the beginning, shows Death
Smilingly over the place,
Trusting this new face.

Bereaved Child's First Night

I've come to close your door, my handsome, my darling,
I've come to close your door and never come again.
The shadow on the ceiling will not be mine, my darling,
So if you wake in terror cry some other name.

There's first time and last, my handsome, my treasure,
No other time, nothing between.
So whenever the hand of darkness clenches on your candle
Shut your eyes, my darling, and slip back into our dream.

STEVIE SMITH

Infelice

Walking swiftly with a dreadful duchess,
He smiled too briefly, his face was as pale as sand,
He jumped into a taxi when he saw me coming,
Leaving me along with a private meaning,
He loves me so much, my heart is singing.
Later at the Club when I rang him in the evening
They said: Sir Rat is dining, is dining, is dining,
No Madam, he left no message, ah how his silence speaks,
He loves me too much for words, my heart is singing.
The Pullman seats are here, the tickets for Paris, I am waiting,
Presently the telephone rings, it is his valet speaking,
Sir Rat is called away, to Scotland, his constituents,
(Ah the dreadful duchess, but he loves me best)
Best pleasure to the last, my heart is singing.
One night he came, it was four in the morning,
Walking slowly upstairs, he stands beside my bed,
Dear darling, lie beside me, it is too cold to stand speaking,
He lies down beside me, his face is like the sand,
He is in a sleep of love, my heart is singing.
Sleeping softly softly, in the morning I must wake him,
And waking he murmurs, I only came to sleep.
The words are so sweetly cruel, how deeply he loves me,
I say them to myself alone, my heart is singing.
Now the sunshine strengthens, it is ten in the morning,
He is so timid in love, he only needs to know,
He is my little child, how can he come if I do not call him,
I will write and tell him everything, I take the pen and write:
I love you so much, my heart is singing.

The Murderer

My true love breathed her latest breath
And I have closed her eyes in death.
It was a cold and windy day
In March, when my love went away.
She was not like other girls – rather diffident,
And that is how we had an accident.

In My Dreams

In my dreams I am always saying goodbye and riding away,
Whither and why I know not nor do I care.
And the parting is sweet and the parting over is sweeter,
And sweetest of all is the night and the rushing air.

In my dreams they are always waving their hands and saying
goodbye,
And they give me the stirrup cup and I smile as I drink,
I am glad the journey is set, I am glad I am going,
I am glad, I am glad, that my friends don't know what I think.

Goodnight

Miriam and Horlick spend a great deal of time putting off going to
bed.
This is the thought that came to me in my bedroom where they
both were, and she said:
Horlick, look at Tuggers, he is getting quite excited in his head.

Tuggers was the dog. And he was getting excited. So.
Miriam had taken her stockings off and you know
Tuggers was getting excited licking her legs, slow, slow.

It's funny Tuggers should be so enthusiastic, said Horlick nastily,
It must be nice to be able to get so excited about nothing really,
Try a little higher up old chap, you're acting puppily.

I yawned. Miriam and Horlick said Goodnight
And went. It was 2 o'clock and Miriam was quite white
With sorrow. Very well then, Goodnight.

Autumn

He told his life story to Mrs Courtly
Who was a widow. 'Let us get married shortly',
He said. 'I am no longer passionate,
But we can have some conversation before it is too late.'

Lady 'Rogue' Singleton

Come, wed me, Lady Singleton,
And we will have a baby soon
And we will live in Edmonton
Where all the friendly people run.

I could never make you happy darling,
Or give you the baby you want,
I would always very much rather, dear,
Live in a tent.

I am not a cold woman, Henry,
But I do not feel for you,
What I feel for the elephants and the miasmas
And the general view.

The River God

I may be smelly and I may be old,
Rough in my pebbles, reedy in my pools,
But where my fish float by I bless their swimming
And I like the people to bathe in me, especially women.
But I can drown the fools
Who bathe too close to the weir, contrary to rules.
And they take a long time drowning
As I throw them up now and then in a spirit of clowning.
Hi yih, yippity-yap, merrily I flow,
O I may be an old foul river but I have plenty of go.
Once there was a lady who was too bold
She bathed in me by the tall black cliff where the water runs cold,
So I brought her down here
To be my beautiful dear.
Oh will she stay with me will she stay
This beautiful lady, or will she go away?
She lies in my beautiful deep river bed with many a weed
To hold her, and many a waving reed.
Oh who would guess what a beautiful white face lies there
Waiting for me to smooth and wash away the fear
She looks at me with.   Hi yih, do not let her
Go.   There is no one one earth who does not forget her
Now.   They say I am a foolish old smelly river
But they do not know of my wide original bed
Where the lady waits, with her golden sleepy head.
If she wishes to go I will not forgive her.

The Deserter

The world is come upon me, I used to keep it a long way off,
But now I have been run over and I am in the hands of the
hospital staff.
They say as a matter of fact I have not been run over it's
imagination,
But they all admit I shall be kept in bed under observation.
I must say it's very comfortable here, nursie has such nice hands,
And every morning the doctor come and lances my tuberculous
glands.
He says he does nothing of the sort, but I have my own feelings
about that,
And what they are if you don't mind I shall keep under my hat.
My friend, if you call it a friend, has left me; he says I am a
deserter to ill health,
And that the things I should think about have made off for ever,
and so has my wealth.
Portentous ass, what to do about him's no strain
I shall quite simply never speak to the fellow again.

Drugs Made Pauline Vague

Drugs made Pauline vague.
She sat one day at the breakfast table
Fingering in a baffled way
The fronds of the maidenhair plant.

Was it the salt you were looking for dear?
Said Dulcie, exchanging a glance with the Brigadier.

Chuff chuff Pauline what's the matter?
Said the Brigadier to his wife
Who did not even notice
What a handsome couple they made.

Not Waving but Drowning

Nobody heard him, the dead man,
But still he lay moaning:
I was much further out than you thought
And not waving but drowning.

Poor chap, he always loved larking
And now he's dead
It must have been too cold for him his heart gave way,
They said.

Oh, no no no, it was too cold always
(Still the dead one lay moaning)
I was much too far out all my life
And not waving but drowning.

The Jungle Husband

Dearest Evelyn, I often think of you
Out with the guns in the jungle stew
Yesterday I hittapotamus
I put the measurements down for you but they got lost in the fuss
It's not a good thing to drink out here
You know, I've practically given it up dear.
Tomorrow I am going alone a long way
Into the jungle.   It is all grey
But green on top
Only sometimes when a tree has fallen
The sun comes down plop, it is quite appalling.
You never want to go in a jungle pool
In the hot sun, it would be the act of a fool
Because it's always full of anacondas, Evelyn, not looking ill-fed
I'll say.   So no more now, from your loving husband, Wilfred.

I Remember

It was my bridal night I remember,
An old man of seventy-three
I lay with my young bride in my arms,
A girl with t.b.
It was wartime, and overhead
The Germans were making a particularly heavy raid on
                                        Hampstead.
What rendered the confusion worse, perversely
Our bombers had chosen that moment to set out for Germany.
Harry, do they ever collide?
I do not think it has ever happened,
Oh my bride, my bride.

A House of Mercy

It was a house of female habitation,
Two ladies fair inhabited the house,
And they were brave. For although Fear knocked loud
Upon the door, and said he must come in,
They did not let him in.

There were also two feeble babes, two girls,
That Mrs S. had by her husband had,
He soon left them and went away to sea,
Nor sent them money, nor came home again
Except to borrow back
Her Naval Officer's Wife's Allowance from Mrs S.
Who gave it him at once, she thought she should.

There was also the ladies' aunt
And babes' great aunt, a Mrs Martha Hearn Clode,
And she was elderly.
These ladies put their money all together
And so we lived.

I was the younger of the feeble babes
And when I was a child my mother died
And later Great Aunt Martha Hearn Clode died
And later still my sister went away.

Now I am old I tend my mother's sister
The noble aunt who so long tended us,
Faithful and True her name is. Tranquil.
Also Sardonic. And I tend the house.

It is a house of female habitation
A house expecting strength as it is strong
A house of aristocratic mould that looks apart
When tears fall; counts despair
Derisory. Yet it has kept us well. For all its faults,
If they are faults, of sternness and reserve,
It is a Being of warmth I think; at heart
A house of mercy.

'The Persian'

The gas fire
Seemed quite a friend
Such a funny little humming noise it made
And it had a name, too, carved on it you know,
'The Persian'. The Persian!
Ha ha ha; ha ha.

Now Agnes, pull yourself together.
You and your friends.

[87]

Scorpion

'This night shall thy soul be required of thee'
My soul is never required of *me*
It always has to be somebody else of course
Will my soul be required of me tonight perhaps?

(I often wonder what it will be like
To have one's soul required of one
But all I can think of is the Out-Patients' Department –
'Are you Mrs Briggs, dear?'
No, I am Scorpion.)

I should like my soul to be required of me, so as
To waft over grass till it comes to the blue sea
I am very fond of grass, I always have been, but there must
Be no cow, person or house to be seen.

Sea and *grass* must be quite empty
Other souls can find somewhere *else*.

O Lord God please come
And require the soul of thy Scorpion

Scorpion so wishes to be gone.

LORINE NIEDECKER

Lake Superior

In every part of every living thing
is stuff that once was rock

In blood the minerals
of the rock

*

Iron the common element of earth
in rocks and freighters

Sault Sainte Marie – big boats
coal-black and iron-ore-red
topped with what white castlework

The waters working together internationally
Gulls playing both sides

*

Radisson:
'a laborinth of pleasure'
this world of the Lake

Long hair, long gun

Fingernails pulled out
by Mohawks

*

                                        (The long
                                          canoes)

'Birch Bark
   and white Seder
     for the ribs'

                         *

Through all this granite land
the sign of the cross

                         *

Beauty: impurities in the rock
And at the blue ice superior spot
priest-robed Marquette grazed
azoic rock, hornblende granite
basalt the common dark
in all the Earth

And his bones of such is coral
raised up out of his grave
were sunned and birch bark-floated
to the straits

                         *

            Joliet
Entered the Mississippi
Found there the paddlebill catfish
come down from The Age of Fishes

At Hudson Bay he conversed in Latin
with an Englishman

To Labrador and back to vanish
His funeral gratis – he'd played
Quebec's Cathedral organ
so many winters

*

Ruby of corundum
lapis lazuli
from changing limestone
glow-apricot red-brown
carnelian sard

Greek named
Exodus-antique
kicked up in America's
Northwest
you have been in my mind
between my toes
agate

*

Wild Pigeon

Did not man
maimed by no
stone-fall

mash the cobalt
and carnelian
of that bird

*

Schoolcraft left the Soo – canoes
US pennants, masts, sails
chanting canoemen, barge
soldiers – for Minnesota

Their South Shore journey
              as if Life's –
The Chocolate River
                The Laughing Fish
and The River of the Dead

Passed peaks of volcanic thrust
Hornblende in massed granite
Wave-cut Cambrian rock
painted by soluble mineral oxides
wave-washed and the rains
did their work and a green
running as from copper

Sea-roaring caverns –
Chippewas threw deermeat
to the savage maws
'*Voyageurs* crossed themselves
tossed a twist of tobacco in'

  Inland then
beside the great granite
gneiss and the schists

to the redolent pondy lakes'
lilies, flag and Indian reed
'through which we successfully passed'

*

[92]

The smooth black stone
I picked up in true source park
    the leaf beside it
once was stone

Why should we hurry
    home

*

I'm sorry to have missed
    Sand Lake
My dear one tells me
    we did not
We watched a gopher there

ROBIN HYDE

from The Beaches

VI

Close under here, I watched two lovers once,
Which should have been a sin, from what you say:
I'd come to look for prawns, small pale-green ghosts,
Sea-coloured bodies tickling round the pool.
But tide was out then; so I strolled away
And climbed the dunes, to lie here warm, face down,
Watching the swimmers by the jetty-posts
And wrinkling like the bright blue wrinkling bay.
It wasn't long before they came; a fool
Could see they had to kiss; but your pet dunce
Didn't quite know men count on more than that;
And so just lay, patterning the sand.
     And they
Were pale thin people, not often clear of town;
Elastic snapped, when he jerked off her hat;
I heard her arguing, 'Dick, my frock!' But he
Thought she was bread.
I wished her legs were brown,
And mostly, then, stared at the dawdling sea,
Hoping Perry would row me some day in his boat.

Not all the time; and when they'd gone, I went
Down to the hollow place where they had been,
Trickling bed through fingers. But I never meant
To tell the rest, or you, what I had seen;
Though that night, when I came in late for tea,
I hoped you'd see the sandgrains on my coat.

E. J. SCOVELL

The Swan's Feet

Who is this whose feet
Close on the water,
Like muscled leaves darker than ivy
Blown back and curved by unwearying wind?
They, that thrust back the water,
Softly crumple now and close, stream in his wake.

These dank weeds are also
Part and plumage of the magnolia-flowering swan.
He puts forth these too –
Leaves of ridged and bitter ivy
Sooted in towns, coal-bright with rain.

He is not moved by winds in air
Like the vain boats on the lake.
Lest you think him too a flower of parchment,
Scentless magnolia,
See his living feet under the water fanning.
In the leaves' self blows the efficient wind
That opens and bends closed those leaves.

The Boy Fishing

I am cold and alone,
On my tree-root sitting as still as stone.
The fish come to my net. I scorned the sun,
The voices on the road, and they have gone.
My eyes are buried in the cold pond, under
The cold, spread leaves; my thoughts are silver-wet.
I have ten stickleback, a half-day's plunder,
Safe in my jar. I shall have ten more yet.

[95]

from The First Year

VII

The days fail: night broods over afternoon:
And at my child's first drink beyond the night
Her skin is silver in the early light.
Sweet the grey morning and the raiders gone.

VIII

The baby in her blue night-jacket, propped on hands
With head raised, coming out to day, has half-way sloughed
The bed-clothes, as a sea-lion, as a mermaid
Half sloughs the sea, rooted in sea, basking on strands.

Like a gentle coastal creature she looks round
At one who comes and goes the far side of her bars;
Firm in her place and lapped by blankets; here like tides
Familiar rise and fall our care for her, our sounds.

ELIZABETH BISHOP

Elizabeth Bishop's executor has requested us to record the fact that the poet objected on principle to appearing in a women's anthology for the following reason, which she stated in a letter dated 8 June, 1977:

Undoubtably gender does play an important part in the making of any art, but art is art and to separate writings, paintings, musical compositions, etc., into two sexes is to emphasize values in them that are *not* art.

The Imaginary Iceberg

We'd rather have the iceberg than the ship,
although it meant the end of travel.
Although it stood stock-still like cloudy rock
and all the sea were moving marble.
We'd rather have the iceberg than the ship;
we'd rather own this breathing plain of snow
though the ship's sails were laid upon the sea
as the snow lies undissolved upon the water.
O solemn, floating field,
are you aware an iceberg takes repose
with you, and when it wakes may pasture on your snows?

This is a scene a sailor'd give his eyes for.
The ship's ignored. The iceberg rises
and sinks again; its glassy pinnacles
correct elliptics in the sky.
This is a scene where he who treads the boards
is artlessly rhetorical. The curtain
is light enough to rise on finest ropes
that airy twists of snow provide.

The wits of these white peaks
spar with the sun. Its weight the iceberg dares
upon a shifting stage and stands and stares.

This iceberg cuts its facets from within.
Like jewelry from a grave
it saves itself perpetually and adorns
only itself, perhaps the snows
which so surprise us lying on the sea.
Good-bye, we say, good-bye, the ship steers off
where waves give in to one another's waves
and clouds run in a warmer sky.
Icebergs behoove the soul
(both being self-made from elements least visible)
to see them so; fleshed, fair, erected indivisible.

Casabianca

Love's the boy stood on the burning deck
trying to recite 'The boy stood on
the burning deck.' Love's the son
    stood stammering elocution
      while the poor ship in flames went down.

Love's the obstinate boy, the ship,
even the swimming sailors, who
would like a schoolroom platform, too,
    or an excuse to stay
      on deck. And love's the burning boy.

Seascape

This celestial seascape, with white herons got up as angels,
flying as high as they want and as far as they want sidewise
in tiers and tiers of immaculate reflections;
the whole region, from the highest heron
down to the weightless mangrove island
with bright green leaves edged neatly with bird-droppings
like illumination in silver,
and down to the suggestively Gothic arches of the mangrove
roots

and the beautiful pea-green back-pasture
where occasionally a fish jumps, like a wild-flower
in an ornamental spray of spray;
this cartoon by Raphael for a tapestry for a Pope:
it does look like heaven.
But a skeletal lighthouse standing there
in black and white clerical dress,
who lives on his nerves, thinks he knows better.
He thinks that hell rages below his iron feet,
that that is why the shallow water is so warm,
and he knows that heaven is not like this.
Heaven is not like flying or swimming,
but has something to do with blackness and a strong glare
and when it gets dark he will remember something
strongly worded to say on the subject.

The Fish

I caught a tremendous fish
and held him beside the boat
half out of water, with my hook
fast in a corner of his mouth.
He didn't fight.
He hadn't fought at all.
He hung a grunting weight,
battered and venerable
and homely. Here and there
his brown skin hung in strips
like ancient wallpaper,
and its pattern of darker brown
was like wallpaper:
shapes like full-blown roses
stained and lost through age.
He was speckled with barnacles,
fine rosettes of lime,
and infested
with tiny white sea-lice,
and underneath two or three
rags of green weed hung down.
While his gills were breathing in
the terrible oxygen
– the frightening gills,
fresh and crisp with blood,
that can cut so badly –
I thought of the coarse white flesh
packed in like feathers,
the big bones and the little bones,
the dramatic reds and blacks
of his shiny entrails,
and the pink swim-bladder
like a big peony.
I looked into his eyes

[100]

which were far larger than mine
but shallower, and yellowed,
the irises backed and packed
with tarnished tinfoil
seen through the lenses
of old scratched isinglass.
They shifted a little, but not
to return my stare.
– It was more like the tipping
of an object toward the light.
I admired his sullen face,
the mechanism of his jaw,
and then I saw
that from his lower lip
– if you could call it a lip –
grim, wet, and weaponlike,
hung five old pieces of fish-line,
or four and a wire leader
with the swivel still attached,
with all their five big hooks
grown firmly in his mouth.
A green line, frayed at the end
where he broke it, two heavier lines,
and a fine black thread
still crimped from the strain and snap
when it broke and he got away.
Like medals with their ribbons
frayed and wavering,
a five-haired beard of wisdom
trailing from his aching jaw.
I stared and stared
and victory filled up
the little rented boat,
from the pool of bilge
where oil had spread a rainbow
around the rusted engine

to the bailer rusted orange,
the sun-cracked thwarts,
the oarlocks on their strings,
the gunnels – until everything
was rainbow, rainbow, rainbow!
And I let the fish go.

Cootchie

Cootchie, Miss Lula's servant, lies in marl,
black into white she went
    below the surface of the coral-reef.
Her life was spent
    in caring for Miss Lula, who is deaf,
eating her dinner off the kitchen sink
while Lula ate hers off the kitchen table.
The skies were egg-white for the funeral
    and the faces sable.

Tonight the moonlight will alleviate
the melting of the pink wax roses
    planted in tin cans filled with sand
placed in a line to mark Miss Lula's losses;
    but who will shout and make her understand?
Searching the land and sea for someone else,
the lighthouse will discover Cootchie's grave
and dismiss all as trivial; the sea, desperate,
    will proffer wave after wave.

Songs for a Colored Singer

I

A washing hangs upon the line,
  but it's not mine.
None of the things that I can see
  belong to me.
The neighbors got a radio with an aerial;
  we got a little portable.
They got a lot of closet space;
  we got a suitcase.

I say, 'Le Roy, just how much are we owing?
Something I can't comprehend,
the more we got the more we spend . . .
He only answers, 'Let's get going.'
Le Roy, you're earning too much money now.

I sit and look at our backyard
  and find it very hard.
What have we got for all his dollars and cents?
  – A pile of bottles by the fence.
He's faithful and he's kind
  but he sure has an inquiring mind.
He's seen a lot; he's bound to see the rest,
  and if I protest

Le Roy answers with a frown,
'Darling, when I earns I spends.
The world is wide; it still extends . . .
I'm going to get a job in the next town.'
Le Roy, you're earning too much money now.

The Bight

On my birthday

At low tide like this how sheer the water is.
White, crumbling ribs of marl protrude and glare
and the boats are dry, the pilings dry as matches.
Absorbing, rather than being absorbed,
the water in the bight doesn't wet anything,
the color of the gas flame turned as low as possible.
One can smell it turning to gas; if one were Baudelaire
one could probably hear it turning to marimba music.
The little ocher dredge at work off the end of the dock
already plays the dry perfectly off-beat claves.
The birds are outsize. Pelicans crash
into this peculiar gas unnecessarily hard,
it seems to me, like pickaxes,
rarely coming up with anything to show for it,
and going off with humorous elbowings.
Black-and-white man-of-war birds soar
on impalpable drafts
and open their tails like scissors on the curves
or tense them like wishbones, till they tremble.
The frowsy sponge boats keep coming in
with the obliging air of retrievers,
bristling with jackstraw gaffs and hooks
and decorated with bobbles of sponges.
There is a fence of chicken wire along the dock
where, glinting like little plowshares,
the blue-gray shark tails are hung up to dry
for the Chinese-restaurant trade.
Some of the little white boats are still piled up
against each other, or lie on their sides, stove in,
and not yet salvaged, if they ever will be, from the last bad storm,
like torn-open, unanswered letters.
The bight is littered with old correspondences.

Click. Click. Goes the dredge,
and brings up a dripping jawful of marl.
All the untidy activity continues,
awful but cheerful.

At the Fishhouses

Although it is a cold evening,
down by one of the fishhouses
an old man sits netting,
his net, in the gloaming almost invisible
a dark purple-brown,
and his shuttle worn and polished.
The air smells so strong of codfish
it makes one's nose run and one's eyes water.
The five fishhouses have steeply peaked roofs
and narrow, cleated gangplanks slant up
to storerooms in the gables
for the wheelbarrows to be pushed up and down on.
All is silver: the heavy surface of the sea,
swelling slowly as if considering spilling over,
is opaque, but the silver of the benches,
the lobster pots, and masts, scattered
among the wild jagged rocks,
is of an apparent translucence
like the small old buildings with an emerald moss
growing on their shoreward walls.
The big fish tubs are completely lined
with layers of beautiful herring scales
and the wheelbarrows are similarly plastered
with creamy iridescent coats of mail,
with small iridescent flies crawling on them.
Up on the little slope behind the houses,
set in the sparse bright sprinkle of grass,
is an ancient wooden capstan,

[105]

cracked, with two long bleached handles
and some melancholy stains, like dried blood,
where the ironwork has rusted.
The old man accepts a Lucky Strike.
He was a friend of my grandfather.
We talk of the decline in the population
and of codfish and herring
while he waits for a herring boat to come in.
There are sequins on his vest and on his thumb.
He has scraped the scales, the principal beauty,
from unnumbered fish with that black old knife,
the blade of which is almost worn away.

Down at the water's edge, at the place
where they haul up the boats, up the long ramp
descending into the water, thin silver
tree trunks are laid horizontally
across the gray stones, down and down
at intervals of four or five feet.

Cold dark deep and absolutely clear,
element bearable to no mortal,
to fish and to seals . . . One seal particularly
I have seen here evening after evening.
He was curious about me. He was interested in music;
like me a believer in total immersion,
so I used to sing him Baptist hymns.
I also sang 'A Mighty Fortress Is Our God.'
He stood up in the water and regarded me
steadily, moving his head a little.
Then he would disappear, then suddenly emerge
almost in the same spot, with a sort of shrug
as if it were against his better judgment.
Cold dark deep and absolutely clear,
the clear gray icy water . . . Back, behind us,
the dignified tall firs begin.

Bluish, associating with their shadows,
a million Christmas trees stand
waiting for Christmas. The water seems suspended
above the rounded gray and blue-gray stones.
I have seen it over and over, the same sea, the same,
slightly, indifferent swinging above the stones,
icily free above the stones,
above the stones and then the world.
If you should dip your hand in,
your wrist would ache immediately,
your bones would begin to ache and your hand would burn
as if the water were a transmutation of fire
that feeds on stones and burns with a dark gray flame.
If you tasted it, it would first taste bitter,
then briny, then surely burn your tongue.
It is like what we imagine knowledge to be:
dark, salt, clear, moving, utterly free,
drawn from the cold hard mouth
of the world, derived from the rocky breasts
forever, flowing and drawn, and since
our knowledge is historical, flowing, and flown.

The Shampoo

The still explosions on the rocks,
the lichens, grow
by spreading, gray, concentric shocks.
They have arranged
to meet the rings around the moon, although
within our memories they have not changed.

And since the heavens will attend
as long on us,
you've been, dear friend,
precipitate and pragmatical;
and look what happens. For Time is
nothing if not amenable.

The shooting stars in your black hair
in bright formation
are flocking where,
so straight, so soon?
– Come, let me wash it in this big tin basin,
battered and shiny like the moon.

Arrival at Santos

Here is a coast; here is a harbor;
here, after a meager diet of horizon, is some scenery:
impractically shaped and – who knows? – self-pitying
                                        mountains,
sad and harsh beneath their frivolous greenery,

with a little church on top of one. And warehouses,
some of them painted a feeble pink, or blue,
and some tall, uncertain palms. Oh, tourist,
is this how this country is going to answer you

and your immodest demands for a different world,
and a better life, and complete comprehension
of both at last, and immediately,
after eighteen days of suspension?

Finish your breakfast. The tender is coming,
a strange and ancient craft, flying a strange and brilliant rag.
So that's the flag. I never saw it before.
I somehow never thought of there *being* a flag,

but of course there was, all along. And coins, I presume,
and paper money; they remain to be seen.
And gingerly now we climb down the ladder backward,
myself and a fellow passenger named Miss Breen,

descending into the midst of twenty-six freighters
waiting to be loaded with green coffee beans.
Please, boy, do be more careful with that boat hook!
Watch out! Oh! It has caught Miss Breen's

skirt! There! Miss Breen is about seventy,
a retired police lieutenant, six feet tall,
with beautiful bright blue eyes and a kind expression.
Her home, when she is at home, is in Glens Fall

s, New York. There. We are settled.
The customs officials will speak English, we hope,
and leave us our bourbon and cigarettes.
Ports are necessities, like postage stamps, or soap,

but they seldom seem to care what impression they make,
or, like this, only attempt, since it does not matter,
the unassertive colors of soap, or postage stamps –
wasting away like the former, slipping the way the latter

do when we mail the letters we wrote on the boat,
either because the glue here is very inferior
or because of the heat. We leave Santos at once;
we are driving to the interior.

Brazil, January 1, 1502

. . . embroidered nature . . . tapestried landscape.
– *Landscape into Art*, by Sir Kenneth Clark

Januaries, Nature greets our eyes
exactly as she must have greeted theirs:
every square inch filling in with foliage –
big leaves, little leaves, and giant leaves,
blue, blue-green, and olive,
with occasional lighter veins and edges,
or a satin underleaf turned over;
monster ferns
in silver-gray relief,
and flowers, too, like giant water lilies
up in the air – up, rather, in the leaves –
purple, yellow, two yellows, pink,
rust red and greenish white;
solid but airy; fresh as if just finished
and taken off the frame.

A blue-white sky, a simple web,
backing for feathery detail:
brief arcs, a pale-green broken wheel,
a few palms, swarthy, squat, but delicate;
and perching there in profile, beaks agape,
the big symbolic birds keep quiet,
each showing only half his puffed and padded,
pure-colored or spotted breast.
Still in the foreground there is Sin:
five sooty dragons near some massy rocks.
The rocks are worked with lichens, gray moonbursts
splattered and overlapping,
threatened from underneath by moss

in lovely hell-green flames,
attacked above
by scaling-ladder vines, oblique and neat,
'one leaf yes and one leaf no' (in Portuguese).
The lizards scarcely breathe; all eyes
are on the smaller, female one, back-to,
her wicked tail straight up and over,
red as a red-hot wire.

Just so the Christians, hard as nails,
tiny as nails, and glinting,
in creaking armor, came and found it all,
not unfamiliar:
no lovers' walks, no bowers,
no cherries to be picked, no lute music,
but corresponding, nevertheless,
to an old dream of wealth and luxury
already out of style when they left home –
wealth, plus a brand-new pleasure.
Directly after Mass, humming perhaps
L'Homme armé or some such tune,
they ripped away into the hanging fabric,
each out to catch an Indian for himself –
those maddening little women who kept calling,
calling to each other (or had the birds waked up?)
and retreating, always retreating, behind it.

Manuelzinho

(Brazil. A friend of the writer is speaking.)

Half squatter, half tenant (no rent) –
a sort of inheritance; white,
in your thirties now, and supposed
to supply me with vegetables,
but you don't; or you won't; or you can't
get the idea through your brain –
the world's worst gardener since Cain.
Tilted above me, your gardens
ravish my eyes. You edge
the beds of silver cabbages
with red carnations, and lettuces
mix with alyssum. And then
umbrella ants arrive,
or it rains for a solid week
and the whole thing's ruined again
and I buy you more pounds of seeds,
imported, guaranteed,
and eventually you bring me
a mystic three-legged carrot,
or a pumpkin 'bigger than the baby'.

I watch you through the rain,
trotting, light, on bare feet,
up the steep paths you have made –
or your father and grandfather made –
all over my property,
with your head and back inside
a sodden burlap bag,
and feel I can't endure it
another minute; then,
indoors, beside the stove,
keep on reading a book.

You steal my telephone wires,
or someone does. You starve
your horse and yourself
and your dogs and family.
Among endless variety,
you eat boiled cabbage stalks.
And once I yelled at you
so loud to hurry up
and fetch me those potatoes
your holey hat flew off,
you jumped out of your clogs,
leaving three objects arranged
in a triangle at me feet,
as if you'd been a gardener
in a fairy tale all this time
and at the word 'potatoes'
had vanished to take up your work
of fairy prince somewhere.

The strangest things happen, to you.
Your cow eats a 'poison grass'
and drops dead on the spot.
Nobody else's does.
And then your father dies,
a superior old man
with a black plush hat, and a moustache
like a white spread-eagled sea gull.
The family gathers, but you,
no, you 'don't think he's dead!
I look at him. He's cold.
They're burying him today.
But you know, I don't think he's *dead*.'
I give you money for the funeral
and you go and hire a *bus*
for the delighted mourners,

so I have to hand over some more
and then have to hear you tell me
you pray for me every night!

And then you come again,
sniffing and shivering,
hat in hand, with that wistful
face, like a child's fistful
of bluets or white violets,
improvident as the dawn,
and once more I provide
for a shot of penicillin
down at the pharmacy, or
one more bottle of
Electrical Baby Syrup.
Or, briskly, you come to settle
what we call our 'accounts',
with two old copybooks,
one with flowers on the cover,
the other with a camel.
Immediate confusion.
You've left out the decimal points.
Your columns stagger,
honeycombed with zeros.
You whisper conspiratorially;
the numbers mount to millions.
Account books? They are Dream Books.
In the kitchen we dream together
how the meek shall inherit the earth –
or several acres of mine.

With blue sugar bags on their heads,
carrying your lunch,
your children scuttle by me
like little moles aboveground,
or even crouch behind bushes

as if I were out to shoot them!
– Impossible to make friends,
though each will grab at once
for an orange or a piece of candy.

Twined in wisps of fog,
I see you all up there
along with Formoso, the donkey,
who brays like a pump gone dry,
then suddenly stops.
– All just standing, staring
off into fog and space.
Or coming down at night,
in silence, except for hoofs,
in dim moonlight, the horse
or Formoso stumbling after.
Between us float a few
big, soft, pale-blue,
sluggish fireflies,
the jellyfish of the air . . .

Patch upon patch upon patch,
your wife keeps all of you covered.
She has gone over and over
(forearmed is forewarned)
your pair of bright-blue pants
with white thread, and these days
your limbs are draped in blueprints.
You paint – heaven knows why –
the outside of the crown
and brim of your straw hat.
Perhaps to reflect the sun?
Or perhaps when you were small,
your mother said, 'Manuelzinho,
one thing: be sure you always
paint your straw hat.'

One was gold for a while,
but the gold wore off, like plate.
One was bright green. Unkindly,
I called you Klorophyll Kid.

My visitors thought it was funny.
I apologize here and now.

You helpless, foolish man,
I love you all I can,
I think. Or do I?
I take off my hat, unpainted
and figurative, to you.
Again I promise to try.

First Death in Nova Scotia

In the cold, cold parlor
my mother laid out Arthur
beneath the chromographs:
Edward, Prince of Wales,
with Princess Alexandra,
and King George with Queen Mary.
Below them on the table
stood a stuffed loon
shot and stuffed by Uncle
Arthur, Arthur's father.

Since Uncle Arthur fired
a bullet into him,
he hadn't said a word.
He kept his own counsel
on his white, frozen lake,
the marble-topped table.
His breast was deep and white,
cold and caressable;
his eyes were red glass,
much to be desired.

'Come,' said my mother,
'Come and say good-bye
to your little cousin Arthur.'
I was lifted up and given
one lily of the valley
to put in Arthur's hand.
Arthur's coffin was
a little frosted cake,
and the red-eyed loon eyed it
from his white, frozen lake.

Arthur was very small.
He was all white, like a doll
that hadn't been painted yet.
Jack Frost had started to paint him
the way he always painted
the Maple Leaf (Forever).
He had just begun on his hair,
a few red strokes, and then
Jack Frost had dropped the brush
and left him white, forever.

The gracious royal couples
were warm in red and ermine;
their feet were well wrapped up
in the ladies' ermine trains.
They invited Arthur to be
the smallest page at court.
But how could Arthur go,
clutching his tiny lily,
with his eyes shut up so tight
and the roads deep in snow?

In the Waiting Room

In Worcester, Massachusetts,
I went with Aunt Consuelo
to keep her dentist's appointment
and sat and waited for her
in the dentist's waiting room.
It was winter. It got dark
early. The waiting room
was full of grown-up people,
arctics and overcoats,
lamps and magazines.
My aunt was inside
what seemed like a long time
and while I waited I read
the *National Geographic*
(I could read) and carefully
studied the photographs:
the inside of a volcano,
black, and full of ashes;
then it was spilling over
in rivulets of fire.
Osa and Martin Johnson
dressed in riding breeches,
laced boots, and pith helmets.
A dead man slung on a pole
– 'Long Pig', the caption said.
Babies with pointed heads
wound round and round with string;
black, naked women with necks
wound round and round with wire
like the necks of light bulbs.
Their breasts were horrifying.
I read it right straight through.
I was too shy to stop.
And then I looked at the cover:
the yellow margins, the date.

Suddenly, from inside,
came an *oh!* of pain
– Aunt Consuelo's voice –
not very loud or long.
I wasn't at all surprised;
even then I knew she was
a foolish, timid woman.
I might have been embarrassed,
but wasn't. What took me
completely by surprise
was that it was *me*:
my voice, in my mouth.
Without thinking at all
I was my foolish aunt,
I – we – were falling, falling,
our eyes glued to the cover
of the *National Geographic*,
February, 1918.

I said to myself: three days
and you'll be seven years old.
I was saying it to stop
the sensation of falling off
the round, turning world
into cold, blue-black space.
But I felt: you are an *I*,
you are an *Elizabeth*,
you are one of *them*.
Why should you be one, too?
I scarcely dared to look
to see what it was I was.
I gave a sidelong glance
– I couldn't look any higher –
at shadowy gray knees,
trousers and skirts and boots
and different pairs of hands

lying under the lamps.
I knew that nothing stranger
had ever happened, that nothing
stranger could ever happen.

Why should I be my aunt,
or me, or anyone?
What similarities –
boots, hands, the family voice
I felt in my throat, or even
the *National Geographic*
and those awful hanging breasts –
held us all together
or made us all just one?
How – I didn't know any
word for it – how 'unlikely' . . .
How had I come to be here,
like them, and overhear
a cry of pain that could have
got loud and worse but hadn't?

The waiting room was bright
and too hot. It was sliding
beneath a big black wave,
another, and another.

Then I was back in it.
The War was on. Outside,
in Worcester, Massachusetts,
were night and slush and cold,
and it was still the fifth
of February, 1918.

The Moose

For Grace Bulmer Bowers

From narrow provinces
of fish and bread and tea,
home of the long tides
where the bay leaves the sea
twice a day and takes
the herrings long rides,

where if the river
enters or retreats
in a wall of brown foam
depends on it if meets
the bay coming in,
the bay not at home;

where, silted red,
sometimes the sun sets
facing a red sea,
and others, veins the flats'
lavender, rich mud
in burning rivulets;

on red, gravelly roads,
down rows of sugar maples,
past clapboard farmhouses
and neat, clapboard churches,
bleached, ridged as clamshells,
past twin silver birches,

through late afternoon
a bus journeys west,
the windshield flashing pink,
pink glancing off of metal,
brushing the dented flank
of blue, beat-up enamel;

[122]

down hollows, up rises,
and waits, patient, while
a lone traveller gives
kisses and embraces
to seven relatives
and a collie supervises.

Goodbye to the elms,
to the farm, to the dog.
The bus starts. The light
grows richer; the fog,
shifting, salty, thin,
comes closing in.

Its cold, round crystals
form and slide and settle
in the white hens' feathers,
in gray glazed cabbages,
on the cabbage roses
and lupins like apostles;

the sweet peas cling
to their wet white string
on the whitewashed fences;
bumblebees creep
inside the foxgloves,
and evening commences.

One stop at Bass River.
Then the Economies –
Lower, Middle, Upper;
Five Islands, Five Houses,
where a woman shakes a tablecloth
out after supper.

A pale flickering. Gone.
The Tantramar marshes
and the smell of salt hay.
An iron bridge trembles
and a loose plank rattles
but doesn't give way.

On the left, a red light
swims through the dark:
a ship's port lantern.
Two rubber boots show,
illuminated, solemn.
A dog gives one bark.

A woman climbs in
with two market bags,
brisk, freckled, elderly.
'A grand night. Yes, sir,
all the way to Boston.'
She regards us amicably.

Moonlight as we enter
the New Brunswick woods,
hairy, scratchy, splintery;
moonlight and mist
caught in them like lamb's wool
on bushes in a pasture.

The passengers lie back.
Snores. Some long sighs.
A dreamy divagation
begins in the night,
a gentle, auditory,
slow hallucination . . .

In the creakings and noises,
an old conversation
– not concerning us,
but recognizable, somewhere,
back in the bus:
Grandparents' voices

uninterruptedly
talking, in Eternity:
names being mentioned,
things cleared up finally;
what he said, what she said,
who got pensioned;

deaths, deaths and sicknesses;
the year he remarried;
the year (something) happened.
She died in childbirth.
That was the son lost
when the schooner foundered.

He took to drink. Yes.
She went to the bad.
When Amos began to pray
even in the store and
finally the family had
to put him away.

'Yes . . .' that peculiar
affirmative. 'Yes . . .'
A sharp, indrawn breath,
half groan, half acceptance,
that means 'Life's like that.
We know *it* (also death).'

Talking the way they talked
in the old featherbed,
peacefully, on and on,
dim lamplight in the hall,
down in the kitchen, the dog
tucked in her shawl.

Now, it's all right now
even to fall asleep
just as on all those nights.
– Suddenly the bus driver
stops with a jolt,
turns off his lights.

A moose has come out of
the impenetrable wood
and stands there, looms, rather,
in the middle of the road.
It approaches; it sniffs at
the bus's hot hood.

Towering, antlerless,
high as a church,
homely as a house
(or, safe as houses).
A man's voice assures us
'Perfectly harmless . . .'

Some of the passengers
exclaim in whispers,
childishly, softly,
'Sure are big creatures.'
'It's awful plain.'
'Look! It's a she!'

Taking her time,
she looks the bus over,
grand, otherworldly.
Why, why do we feel
(we all feel) this sweet
sensation of joy?

'Curious creatures,'
says our quiet driver,
rolling his *r*'s.
'Look at that, would you.'
Then he shifts gears.
For a moment longer,

by craning backward,
the moose can be seen
on the moonlit macadam;
then there's a dim
smell of moose, an acrid
smell of gasoline.

JOSEPHINE MILES

Dolor

When swimming and croquet are in full sway, dolor
Asserts itself, rocks on the porches its own whited color.

Dolor dismayed with one life after another
Tells its tally, but never tells enough.

Never gets the last iota pat, never gets
Veronica buried, thought of her too late.

Extend, dolor, extend, assert, and let
No one walk to the post office in the middle of this.

Maintain on one sun porch, in one mild
Summer, one dismay unreconciled.

The Day the Winds

The day the winds went underground I gasped for breath,
Did not you? – oxygen gone from the chest wall,
Nostrils pinched in the scant weather, strictest
Sort of equilibrium at street corners.

It was a pity. Who could walk in the hills now
Or run for a train? The water in a storm
Ran down the sides of buildings and the bark of trees
Straight down, like tears.

In the first days it was not so desperate;
I remember, though short of breath,
Thinking with relief in the dense quiet,
Fall will be quiet.

But more and more as the streets clogged with traffic
And the smog of the city's production lay on its eyes,
One could notice persons burrowing, hearts hammering,
Toward the risks of the wind.

Summer

When I came to show you my summer cottage
By the resounding sea,
We found a housing project building around it,
Two stories being painted green row after row
So we were set in an alley.

But there is the sea I said, off the far corner
Through that vacant land;
And there the pile of prefabricating panels
And the cement blocks swiftly
Rose in the sand.

So darkened the sunlit alley.
Ovid, Arthur, oh Orion I said, run
Take Rags with you, send me back
News of the sea.
So they did, vanishing away off and shouting.

Belief

Mother said to call her if the H bomb exploded
And I said I would, and it about did
When Louis my brother robbed a service station
And lay cursing on the oily cement in handcuffs.

But by that time it was too late to tell Mother,
She was too sick to worry the life out of her
Over *why why*. Causation is sequence
And everything is one thing after another.

Besides, my other brother, Eddie, had got to be President,
And you can't ask too much of one family.
The chances were as good for a good future
As bad for a bad one.

Therefore it was surprising that, as we kept the newspapers from
Mother,
She died feeling responsible for a disaster unverified,
Murmuring, in her sleep as it seemed, the ancient slogan
Noblesse oblige.

Ride

It's not my world, I grant, but I made it.
It's not my ranch, lean oak, buzzard crow,
Not my fryers, mixmaster, well-garden.
And now it's down the road and I made it.

It's not your rackety car but you drive it.
It's not your four-door, top-speed, white-wall tires,
Not our state, not even, I guess, our nation,
But now it's down the road, and we're in it.

Bibliographer

Bad quartos were my first love.
Ever since,
I have worked in the particular possession
Of their providence.

Though increasingly wild the world
And as death corrupt,
My first love brings me succor
As I learn its script.

So that, in my presence,
Rank and complete
Spoil and error
Are not really dissolute.

I will take them up
And gently gent-
Ly love them, tell them
What they have probably meant.

Conception

Death did not come to my mother
Like an old friend.
She was a mother, and she must
Conceive him.

Up and down the bed she fought crying
Help me, but death
Was a slow child
Heavy. He

[131]

Waited. When he was born
We took and tired him, now he is ready
To do his good in the world.

He has my mother's features.
He can go among strangers
To save lives.

Family

When you swim in the surf off Seal Rocks, and your family
Sits in the sand
Eating potato salad, and the undertow
Comes which takes you out away down
To loss of breath loss of play and the power of play
Holler, say
Help, help, help. Hello, they will say,
Come back here for some potato salad.

It is then that a seventeen-year-old cub
Cruising in a helicopter from Antigua,
A jackstraw expert speaking only Swedish
And remote from this area as a camel, says
Look down there, there is somebody drowning.

And it is you. You say, yes, yes,
And he throws you a line.
This is what is called the brotherhood of man.

Album

This is a hard life you are living
While you are young,
My father said,
As I scratched my casted knees with a paper knife.
By laws of compensation
Your old age should be grand.

Not grand, but of a terrible
Compensation, to perceive
Past the energy of survival
In its sadness
The hard life of the young.

Officers

Mr Hansen, the cop at the campus gate,
Put me through college.
While the dean of women
Advised against it, too complicated, the cop said,
You get enrolled some way, and I'll let you in.
Every morning, four years. On commencement day
I showed him my diploma.

Later when radio news announced Clark Kerr
President, my first rejoicing
Was with Mr Taylor
At the campus gate. He shook hands
Joyfully, as I went in to a Marianne Moore reading.
And we exchanged over many years
Varying views of the weather.

[133]

Then on a dark night a giant officer came up to the car
When we were going to a senate meeting, strikebound by pickets,
And smashed his billy club down on the elbow of my student driver.
Where do you think you're going? I suddenly saw I knew him.
It's you, Mr Graham, I mean it's us, going to the meeting. He
walked away,
Turning short and small, which he was, a compact man
Of great neatness.

Later when I taught in the basement corridor,
The fuzz came through,
Running, loosing tear-gas bombs in the corridor
To rise and choke in offices and classrooms,
Too late for escape. Their gas masks distorted their appearance
But they were Mr O'Neill and Mr Swenson.

Since then, I have not met an officer
That I can call by name.

MURIEL RUKEYSER

Then I Saw What the Calling Was

All the voices of the wood called 'Muriel!'
but it was soon solved;   it was nothing, it was not for me.
The words were a little like Mortal and More and Endure
and a word like Real, a sound like Health or Hell.
Then I saw what the calling was   :   it was the road I traveled,
                                                                the clear
time and these colors of orchards, gold behind gold and the full
shadow behind each tree and behind each slope.   Not to me
the calling, but to anyone, and at last I saw   :   where
the road lay through sunlight and many voices and the marvel
orchards, not for me, not for me, not for me.
I came into my clear being;   uncalled, alive, and sure.
Nothing was speaking to me, but I offered and all was well.

And then I arrived at the powerful green hill.

Myth

Long afterward, Oedipus, old and blinded, walked the
roads.   He smelled a familiar smell.   It was
the Sphinx.   Oedipus said, 'I want to ask one question.
Why didn't I recognize my mother?'   'You gave the
wrong answer,' said the Sphinx.   'But that was what
made everything possible,' said Oedipus.   'No,' she said.
'When I asked, What walks on four legs in the morning,
two at noon, and three in the evening, you answered,
Man.   You didn't say anything about woman.'
'When you say Man,' said Oedipus, 'you include women
too. Everyone knows that.'   She said, 'That's what
you think.'

[135]

JUDITH WRIGHT

Brother and Sisters

The road turned out to be a cul-de-sac;
stopped like a lost intention at the gate
and never crossed the mountains to the coast.
But they stayed on. Years grew like grass and leaves
across the half-erased and dubious track
until one day they knew the plans were lost,
the blueprint for the bridge was out of date,
and now their orchards never would be planted.
The saplings sprouted slyly; day by day
the bush moved one step nearer, wondering when.
The polished parlour grew *distrait* and haunted
where Millie, Lucy, John each night at ten
wound the gilt clock that leaked the year away.

The pianola – oh, listen to the mocking bird –
wavers on Sundays and has lost a note.
The wrinkled ewes snatch pansies through the fence
and stare with shallow eyes into the garden
where Lucy shrivels waiting for a word,
and Millie's cameos loosen round her throat.
The bush comes near, the ranges grow immense.

Feeding the lambs deserted in early spring
Lucy looked up and saw the stockman's eye
telling her she was cracked and old.

                        The wall
groans in the night and settles more awry.
O how they lie awake. Their thoughts go fluttering
from room to room like moths: 'Millie, are you awake?'
'Oh John, I have been dreaming.' 'Lucy, do you cry?'
– meet tentative as moths. Antennae stroke a wing.
'There is nothing to be afraid of. Nothing at all.'

[136]

South of My Days

South of my days' circle, part of my blood's country,
rises that tableland, high delicate outline
of bony slopes wincing under the winter,
low trees blue-leaved and olive, outcropping granite –
clean, lean, hungry country. The creek's leaf-silenced,
willow-choked, the slope a tangle of medlar and crab-apple
branching over and under, blotched with a green lichen;
and the old cottage lurches in for shelter.

O cold the black-frost night. The walls draw in to the warmth
and the old roof cracks its joints; the slung kettle
hisses a leak on the fire. Hardly to be believed that summer
will turn up again some day in a wave of rambler roses,
thrust its hot face in here to tell another yarn –
a story old Dan can spin into a blanket against the winter.
Seventy years of stories he clutches round his bones.
Seventy summers are hived in him like old honey.

Droving that year, Charleville to the Hunter,
nineteen-one it was, and the drought beginning;
sixty head left at the McIntyre, the mud round them
hardened like iron; and the yellow boy died
in the sulky ahead with the gear, but the horse went on,
stopped at the Sandy Camp and waited in the evening.
It was the flies we seen first, swarming like bees.
Came to the Hunter, three hundred head of a thousand –
cruel to keep them alive – and the river was dust.

Or mustering up in the Bogongs in the autumn
when the blizzards came early. Brought them down; we brought
them
down, what aren't there yet. Or driving for Cobb's on the run
up from Tamworth – Thunderbolt at the top of Hungry Hill,

and I give him a wink. I wouldn't wait long, Fred,
not if I was you; the troopers are just behind,
coming for that job at the Hillgrove. He went like a luny,
him on his big black horse.

       Oh, they slide and they vanish
as he shuffles the years like a pack of conjuror's cards.
True or not, it's all the same; and the frost on the roof
cracks like a whip, and the back-log breaks into ash.
Wake, old man. This is winter, and the yarns are over.
No one is listening.
       South of my days' circle
I know it dark against the stars, the high lean country
full of old stories that still go walking in my sleep.

The Cup

Silence is harder, Una said.
If I could be quiet I might come true
like the blue cup hung over the sink,
which is not dead,
but waiting for someone to fill it and drink.

Una said, Silence can reach my mouth:
but a long way in my trouble lies.
The look in my eyes, the sound of my words
all tell the truth:
they spring from my trouble like a flight of birds.

Let silence travel, Una said,
by every track of nerve and vein
to heart and brain, where the troubles begin.
Then I shan't be dead,
but waiting for something to come in.

[138]

Request to a Year

If the year is meditating a suitable gift,
I should like it to be the attitude
of my great-great-grandmother,
legendary devotee of the arts,

who, having had eight children
and little opportunity for painting pictures,
sat one day on a high rock
beside a river in Switzerland

and from a difficult distance viewed
her second son, balanced on a small ice-floe,
drift down the current towards a waterfall
that struck rock-bottom eighty feet below,

while her second daughter, impeded,
no doubt, by the petticoats of the day,
stretched out a last-hope alpenstock
(which luckily later caught him on his way).

Nothing, it was evident, could be done;
and with the artist's isolating eye
my great-great-grandmother hastily sketched the scene.
The sketch survives to prove the story by.

Year, if you have no Mother's day present planned;
reach back and bring me the firmness of her hand.

GWENDOLYN BROOKS

Kitchenette Building

We are things of dry hours and the involuntary plan,
Grayed in, and gray. 'Dream' makes a giddy sound, not strong
Like 'rent', 'feeding a wife', 'satisfying a man'.

But could a dream send up through onion fumes
Its white and violet, fight with fried potatoes
And yesterday's garbage ripening in the hall,
Flutter, or sing an aria down these rooms

Even if we were willing to let it in,
Had time to warm it, keep it very clean,
Anticipate a message, let it begin?

We wonder. But not well! not for a minute!
Since Number Five is out of the bathroom now,
We think of lukewarm water, hope to get in it.

The Mother

Abortions will not let you forget.
You remember the children you got that you did not get,
The damp small pulps with a little or with no hair,
The singers and workers that never handled the air.
You will never neglect or beat
Them, or silence or buy with a sweet.
You will never wind up the sucking-thumb
Or scuttle off ghosts that come.
You will never leave them, controlling your luscious sigh,
Return for a snack of them, with gobbling mother-eye.

I have heard in the voices of the wind the voices of my dim killed
children.

I have contracted. I have eased
My dim dears at the breasts they could never suck.
I have said, Sweets, if I sinned, if I seized
Your luck
And your lives from your unfinished reach,
If I stole your births and your names,
Your straight baby tears and your games,
Your stilted or lovely loves, your tumults, your marriages, aches,
and your deaths,
If I poisoned the beginnings of your breaths,
Believe that even in my deliberateness I was not deliberate.
Though why should I whine,
Whine that the crime was other than mine? –
Since anyhow you are dead.
Or rather, or instead,
You were never made.
But that too, I am afraid,
Is faulty: oh, what shall I say, how is the truth to be said?
You were born, you had body, you died.
It is just that you never giggled or planned or cried.

Believe me, I loved you all.
Believe me, I knew you, though faintly, and I loved, I loved you
All.

A Sunset of the City

Kathleen Eileen

Already I am no longer looked at with lechery or love.
My daughters and sons have put me away with marbles and dolls,
Are gone from the house.
My husband and lovers are pleasant or somewhat polite
And night is night.

It is a real chill out,
The genuine thing.
I am not deceived, I do not think it is still summer
Because sun stays and birds continue to sing.

It is summer-gone that I see, it is summer-gone.
The sweet flowers indrying and dying down,
The grasses forgetting their blaze and consenting to brown.

It is a real chill out. The fall crisp comes.
I am aware there is winter to heed.
There is no warm house
That is fitted with my need.

I am cold in this cold house this house
Whose washed echoes are tremulous down lost halls.
I am a woman, and dusty, standing among new affairs.
I am a woman who hurries through her prayers.

Tin intimations of a quiet core to be my
Desert and my dear relief
Come: there shall be such islanding from grief,
And small communion with the master shore.
Twang they. And I incline this ear to tin,
Consult a dual dilemma. Whether to dry
In humming pallor or to leap and die.

Somebody muffed it? Somebody wanted to joke.

[142]

P. K. PAGE

Brazilian Fazenda

That day all the slaves were freed
their manacles, anklets
left on the window ledge to rust in the moist air

and all the coffee ripened
like beads on a bush or balls of fire
as merry as Christmas

and the cows all calved and the calves all lived
such a moo.

On the wide verandah where birds in cages
sang among the bell flowers
I in a bridal hammock
white and tasselled
whistled

and bits fell out of the sky near Nossa Senhora
who had walked all the way in bare feet from Bahia

and the chapel was lit by a child's
fistful of marigolds on the red velvet altar
thrown like a golden ball.

Oh let me come back on a day
when nothing extraordinary happens
so I can stare
at the sugar white pillars
and black lace grills
of this pink house.

MARGARET AVISON

Thaw

Sticky inside their winter suits
the Sunday children stare at pools
in pavement and black ice where roots
of sky in moodier sky dissolve.

   An empty coach train runs along
   the thin and sooty river flats
   and stick and straw and random stones
   steam faintly when its steam departs.

Lime-water and licorice light
wander the tumbled streets. A few
sparrows gather. A dog barks out
under the dogless pale pale blue.

   Move your tongue along a slat
   of raspberry box from last year's crate.
   Smell a saucepantilt of water
   on the coal-ash in your grate.

Think how the Black Death made men dance,
and from the silt of centuries
the proof is now scraped bare that once
Troy fell and Pompeii scorched and froze.

   A boy alone out in the court
   whacks with his hockey stick, and whacks
   in the wet, and the pigeons flutter, and rise,
   and settle back.

Transit

Blowing hard at the bus stop:
south-bound, NW corner.
Barometer falling.
Stars falling, but in that
blue sky who marks it, they fall all over out there.

Wind's off the Barren Straits.
But the sun is blowing too.
Reared high out of the nest
snakeheads flap in it till the
tear ducts crackle.

The whole geste unrolls; black cars,
poles, black-&-white headlines,
dentist's floss, wire-mesh,
heads spinning, and
a thorn needle for every solitary tune even though there's no
automatic arm. And it's
all plugged in
and everything's coming.
But the bus isn't coming.

Noon keeps swallowing.

ELMA MITCHELL

Thoughts After Ruskin

Women reminded him of lilies and roses.
Me they remind rather of blood and soap,
Armed with a warm rag, assaulting noses,
Ears, neck, mouth and all the secret places:

Armed with a sharp knife, cutting up liver,
Holding hearts to bleed under a running tap,
Gutting and stuffing, pickling and preserving,
Scalding, blanching, broiling, pulverizing,
– All the terrible chemistry of their kitchens.

Their distant husbands lean across mahogany
And delicately manipulate the market,
While safe at home, the tender and the gentle
Are killing tiny mice, dead snap by the neck,
Asphyxiating flies, evicting spiders,
Scrubbing, scouring aloud, disturbing cupboards,
Committing things to dustbins, twisting, wringing,
Wrists red and knuckles white and fingers puckered,
Pulpy, tepid. Steering screaming cleaners
Arounds the snags of furniture, they straighten
And haul out sheets from under the incontinent
And heavy old, stoop to importunate young,
Tugging, folding, tucking, zipping, buttoning,
Spooning in food, encouraging excretion,
Mopping up vomit, stabbing cloth with needles,
Contorting wool around their knitting needles,
Creating snug and comfy on their needles.

[146]

Their huge hands! their everywhere eyes! their voices
Raised to convey across the hullabaloo,
Their massive thighs and breasts dispensing comfort,
Their bloody passages and hairy crannies,
Their wombs that pocket a man upside down!

And when all's over, off with overalls,
Quickly consulting clocks, they go upstairs,
Sit and sigh a little, brushing hair,
And somehow find, in mirrors, colours, odours,
Their essences of lilies and of roses.

MAY SWENSON

The Centaur

The summer that I was ten –
Can it be there was only one
summer that I was ten? It must

have been a long one then –
each day I'd go out to choose
a fresh horse from my stable

which was a willow grove
down by the old canal.
I'd go on my two bare feet.

But when, with my brother's jack-knife,
I had cut me a long limber horse
with a good thick knob for a head,

and peeled him slick and clean
except a few leaves for the tail,
and cinched my brother's belt

around his head for a rein,
I'd straddle and canter him fast
up the grass bank to the path,

trot along in the lovely dust
that talcumed over his hoofs,
hiding my toes, and turning

his feet to swift half-moons.
The willow knob with the strap
jouncing between my thighs

[148]

was the pommel and yet the poll
of my nickering pony's head.
My head and my neck were mine,

yet they were shaped like a horse.
My hair flopped to the side
like the mane of a horse in the wind.

My forelock swung in my eyes,
my neck arched and I snorted.
I shied and skittered and reared,

stopped and raised my knees,
pawed at the ground and quivered.
My teeth bared as we wheeled

and swished through the dust again.
I was the horse and the rider,
and the leather I slapped to his rump

spanked my own behind.
Doubled, my two hoofs beat
a gallop along the bank,

the wind twanged in my mane,
my mouth squared to the bit.
And yet I sat on my steed

quiet, negligent riding,
my toes standing the stirrups,
my thighs hugging his ribs.

At a walk we drew up to the porch.
I tethered him to a paling.
Dismounting, I smoothed my skirt

and entered the dusky hall.
My feet on the clean linoleum
left ghostly toes in the hall.

Where have you been? said my mother.
Been riding, I said from the sink,
and filled me a glass of water.

What's that in your pocket? she said.
Just my knife. It weighted my pocket
and stretched my dress awry.

Go tie back your hair, said my mother,
and *Why is your mouth all green?*
*Rob Roy, he pulled some clover
as we crossed the field,* I told her.

The James Bond Movie

The popcorn is greasy, and I forgot to bring a Kleenex.
A pill that's a bomb inside the stomach of a man inside

The Embassy blows up. Eructations of flame, luxurious
cauliflowers giganticize into motion. The entire 29-ft.

screen is orange, is crackling flesh and brick bursting,
blackening, smithereened. I unwrap a Dentyne and, while

jouncing my teeth in rubber tongue-smarting clove, try
with the 2-inch-wide paper to blot butter off my fingers.

A bubble-bath, room-sized, in which 14 girls, delectable
and sexless, twist-topped Creamy Freezes (their blonde,

red, brown, pinkish, lavender or silver wiglets all
screwed that high, and varnished), scrub-tickle a lone

male, whose chest has just the right amount and distribu-
tion of curly hair. He's nervously pretending to defend

his modesty. His crotch, below the waterline, is also
below the frame – but unsubmerged all 28 slick foamy boobs.

Their makeup fails to let the girls look naked. Caterpil-
lar lashes, black and thick, lush lips glossed pink like

the gum I pop and chew, contact lenses on the eyes that are
mostly blue, they're nose-perfect replicas of each other.

I've got most of the grease off and onto this little square
of paper. I'm folding it now, making creases with my nails.

AMY CLAMPITT

Beach Glass

While you walk the water's edge,
turning over concepts
I can't envision, the honking buoy
serves notice that at any time
the wind may change,
the reef-bell clatters
its treble monotone, deaf as Cassandra
to any note but warning. The ocean,
cumbered by no business more urgent
than keeping open old accounts
that never balanced,
goes on shuffling its millenniums
of quartz, granite, basalt.
                              It behaves
toward the permutations of novelty –
driftwood and shipwreck, last night's
beer cans, spilt oil, the coughed-up
residue of plastic – with random
impartiality, playing catch or tag
or touch-last like a terrier,
turning the same thing over and over,
over and over. For the ocean, nothing
is beneath consideration.

                              The houses
of so many mussels and periwinkles
have been abandoned here, it's hopeless
to know which to salvage. Instead
I keep a lookout for beach glass –
amber of Budweiser, chrysoprase
of Almadén and Gallo, lapis

by way of (no getting around it,
I'm afraid) Phillips'
Milk of Magnesia, with now and then a rare
translucent turquoise or blurred amethyst
of no known origin.
                    The process
goes on forever: they came from sand,
they go back to gravel,
along with the treasuries
of Murano, the buttressed
astonishments of Chartres,
which even now are readying
for being turned over and over as gravely
and gradually as an intellect
engaged in the hazardous
redefinition of structures
no one has yet looked at.

A Procession at Candlemas

1

Moving on or going back to where you came from,
bad news is what you mainly travel with:
a breakup or a breakdown, someone running off

or walking out, called up or called home:
death in the family. Nudged from their stanchions
outside the terminal, anonymous of purpose

as a flock of birds, the bison of the highway
funnel westward onto Route 80, mirroring
an entity that cannot look into itself and know

what makes it what it is. Sooner or later
every trek becomes a funeral procession.
The mother curtained in Intensive Care –

a scene the mind leaves blank, fleeing instead
toward scenes of transhumance, the belled sheep
moving up the Pyrenees, red-tasseled pack llamas

footing velvet-green precipices, the Kurdish
women, jingling with bangles, gorgeous
on their rug-piled mounts – already lying dead,

bereavement altering the moving lights
to a processional, a feast of Candlemas.
Change as child-bearing, birth as a kind

of shucking off: out of what began
as a Mosaic insult – such a loathing
of the common origin, even a virgin,

having given birth, needs purifying –
to carry fire as though it were a flower,
the terror and the loveliness entrusted

into naked hands, supposing God might have,
might actually need a mother: people have
at times found this a way of being happy.

A Candlemas of moving lights along Route 80;
lighted candles in a corridor from Arlington
over the Potomac, for every carried flame

the name of a dead soldier: an element
fragile as ego, frightening as parturition,
necessary and intractable as dreaming.

The lapped, wheelborne integument, layer
within layer, at the core a dream of
something precious, ripped: Where are we?

The sleepers groan, stir, rewrap themselves
about the self's imponderable substance,
or clamber down, numb-footed, half in a drowse

of freezing dark, through a Stonehenge
of fuel pumps, the bison hulks slantwise
beside them, drinking. What is real except

what's fabricated? The jellies glitter
cream-capped in the cafeteria showcase;
gumball globes, Life Savers cinctured

in parcel gilt, plop from their housings
perfect, like miracles. Comb, nail clipper,
lip rouge, mirrors and emollients embody,

niched into the washroom wall case,
the pristine seductiveness of money.
Absently, without inhabitants, this

nowhere oasis wears the place name
of Indian Meadows. The westward-trekking
transhumance, once only, of a people who,

in losing everything they had, lost even
the names they went by, stumbling past
like caribou, perhaps camped here. Who

can assign a trade-in value to that sorrow?
The monk in sheepskin over tucked-up saffron
intoning to a drum becomes the metronome

of one more straggle up Pennsylvania Avenue
in falling snow, a whirl of tenderly
remorseless corpuscles, street gangs

[155]

amok among magnolias' pregnant wands,
a stillness at the heart of so much whirling:
beyond the torn integument of childbirth,

sometimes, wrapped like a papoose into a grief
not merely of the ego, you rediscover almost
the rest-in-peace of the placental coracle.

2

Of what the dead were, living, one knows
so little as barely to recognize
the fabric of the backward-ramifying

antecedents, half-noted presences
in darkened rooms: the old, the feared,
the hallowed. Never the same river

drowns the unalterable doorsill. An effigy
in olive wood or pear wood, dank
with the sweat of age, walled in the dark

at Brauron, Argos, Samos: even the unwed
Athene, who had no mother, born – it's declared –
of some man's brain like every other pure idea,

had her own wizened cult object, kept
out of sight like the incontinent whimperer
in the backstairs bedrooms, where no child

ever goes – to whom, year after year,
the fair linen of the sacred peplos
was brought in ceremonial procession –

flutes and stringed instruments, wildflower-
hung cattle, nubile Athenian girls, young men
praised for the beauty of their bodies. Who

can unpeel the layers of that seasonal
returning to the dark where memory fails,
as birds re-enter the ancestral flyway?

Daylight, snow falling, knotting of gears:
Chicago. Soot, the rotting backsides
of tenements, grimed trollshapes of ice

underneath the bridges, the tunnel heaving
like a birth canal. Disgorged, the infant
howling in the restroom; steam-table cereal,

pale coffee; wall-eyed TV receivers, armchairs
of molded plastic: the squalor of the day
resumed, the orphaned litter taken up again

unloved, the spawn of botched intentions,
grief a mere hardening of the gut,
a set piece of what can't be avoided:

parents by the tens of thousands living
unthanked, unpaid but in the sour coin
of resentment. Midmorning gray as zinc

along Route 80, corn-stubble quilting
the underside of snowdrifts, the cadaverous
belvedere of windmills, the sullen stare

of feedlot cattle; black creeks puncturing
white terrain, the frozen bottomland
a mush of willow tops; dragnetted in ice,

the Mississippi. Westward toward the dark,
the undertow of scenes come back to, fright
riddling the structures of interior history:

Where is it? Where, in the shucked-off
bundle, the hampered obscurity that has been
for centuries the mumbling lot of women,

did the thread of fire, too frail
ever to discover what it meant, to risk
even the taking of a shape, relinquish

the seed of possibility, unguessed-at
as a dream of something precious? Memory,
that exquisite blunderer, stumbling

like a migrant bird that finds the flyway
it hardly knew it knew except by instinct,
down the long-unentered nave of childhood,

late on a midwinter afternoon, alone
among the snow-hung hollows of the windbreak
on the far side of the orchard, encounters

sheltering among the evergreens, a small
stilled bird, its cap of clear yellow
slit by a thread of scarlet – the untouched

nucleus of fire, the lost connection
hallowing the wizened effigy, the mother
curtained in Intensive Care: a Candlemas

of moving lights along Route 80, at nightfall,
in falling snow, the stillness and the sorrow
of things moving back to where they came from.

What the Light Was Like

For Louise Dickinson Rich
and the family of Ernest Woodward

Every year in June – up here, that's the month for lilacs –
    almost his whole front yard,
with lobster traps stacked out in back, atop the rise
    that overlooks the inlet
would be a Himalayan range of peaks of bloom,
    white or mauve-violet,

gusting a turbulence of perfume, and every year the same
    iridescent hummingbird,
or its descendant, would be at work among the mourning cloaks
    and swallowtails, its motor loud,
its burning gorget darkening at moments as though charred.
    He kept an eye out

for it, we learned one evening, as for everything that flapped
    or hopped or hovered
crepuscular under the firs: he'd heard the legendary
    trilling of the woodcock,
and watched the eiders, once rare along these coasts,
    making their comeback

so that now they're everywhere, in tribes, in families
    of aunts and cousins,
a knit-and-purl of irresistibly downy young behind them, riding
    every cove and inlet;
and yes, in answer to the question summer people always ask,
    he'd seen the puffins

that breed out on 'Tit Manan, in summer improbably clown-faced
    behind the striped scarlet
of Commedia dell' Arte masks we'll never see except in
    Roger Tory Peterson's
field guide, or childish wishful thinking. There was much
    else I meant to ask about

another summer. But in June, when we came limping up here
    again, looking forward
to easing up from a mean, hard, unaccommodating winter,
    we heard how he'd gone out
at dawn, one morning in October, unmoored the dinghy
    and rowed to his boat

as usual, the harbor already chugging with half a dozen
    neighbors' revved-up craft,
wet decks stacked abaft with traps, the bait and kegs stowed
    forward, a lifting weft
of fog spooled off in pearl-pink fleeces overhead with the first
    daylight, and steered,

as usual, past first the inner and then the outer bar, where in
    whatever kind of weather,
the red reef-bell yells, in that interminable treble, *Trouble*,
    out past where the Groaner
lolls, its tempo and forte changing with the chop, played on
    by every wind shift,

straight into the sunrise, a surge of burning turning the
    whole ocean iridescent
fool's-gold over molten emerald, into the core of that
    day-after-day amazement –
a clue, one must suppose, to why lobstermen are often
    naturally gracious:

maybe, out there beside the wheel, the Baptist spire
    shrunk to a compass-
point, the town an interrupted circlet, feeble as an apron-
    string, for all the labor
it took to put it there, it's finding, out in that ungirdled
    wallowing and glitter,

finally, that what you love most is the same as what you're
    most afraid of – God,
in a word; whereas it seems they think they've got it licked
    (or used to), back there
in the Restricted Area for instance, where that huge hush-
    hush thing they say is radar

sits sprawling on the heath like Stonehenge, belittling every
    other man-made thing
in view, even the gargantuan pods of the new boat hulls you
    now and then see lying,
stark naked, crimson on the inside as a just-skinned carcass,
    in Young's boatyard,

even the gray Grange Hall, wood-heated by a yardarm of
                                                    stovepipe
    across the ceiling.
Out there, from that wallowing perspective, all comparisons
    amount to nothing,
though once you've hauled your last trap, things tend to wander
    into shorter focus

as, around noon, you head back in: first 'Tit Manan lighthouse,
    a ghostly gimlet
on its ledge by day, but on clear nights expanding to a
    shout, to starboard,
the sunstruck rock pile of Cranberry Point to port; then
    you see the hamlet

rainbowed, above the blurring of the spray shield, by the
    hurrying herring gulls'
insatiable fandango of excitement – the spire first, then
    the crimson boat hulls,
the struts of the ill-natured gadget on the heath behind them
    as the face of things expands,

the hide-and-seek behind the velvet-shouldered, sparse
    tree-spined profiles,
as first the outer, then the inner bar appears, then the scree-
    beach under Crowley Island's
crowding firs and spruces, and you detect among the chimneys
    and the TV aerials,

yours. But by mid-afternoon of that October day,
    when all his neighbors'
boats had chugged back through the inlet, his
    was still out; at evening,
with half the town out looking, and a hard frost
    settling in among the alders,

there'd been no sign of him. The next day, and the next,
    the search went on,
and widened, joined by planes and helicopters from as
    far away as Boston.
When, on the third day, his craft was sighted
    finally, it had drifted,

with its engine running, till the last gulp of fuel
    spluttered and ran out,
beyond the town's own speckled noose of buoys, past
    the furred crest of Schoodic,
vivid in a skirt of aspens, the boglands cranberry-
    crimson at its foot,

[162]

past the bald brow the sunrise always strikes first, of
    the hulk of Cadillac,
riding the current effortlessly as eiders tied to water
    by the summer molt,
for fifty miles southwestward to where, off Matinicus,
    out past the rock

that, like 'Tit Manan, is a restricted area, off limits for
    all purposes but puffins',
they spotted him, slumped against the kegs. I find it
    tempting to imagine what,
when the blood roared, overflowing its cerebral sluiceway,
    and the iridescence

of his last perception, charring, gave way to unreversed,
    irrevocable dark,
the light out there was like, that's always shifting – from
    a nimbus gone berserk
to a single gorget, a cathedral train of blinking, or
    the fogbound shroud

that can turn anywhere into a nowhere. But it's useless.
    Among the mourning-cloak-
hovered-over lilac peaks, their whites and purples,
    when we pass his yard,
poignant to excess with fragrance, this year we haven't
    seen the hummingbird.

ROSEMARY DOBSON

Country Press

Under the dusty print of hobnailed boot,
Strewn on the floor the papers still assert
In ornamental gothic, swash italics
And bands of printer's flowers (traditional)
Mixed in a riot of typographic fancy,
This is the *Western Star*, the Farmer's Guide,
The Voice of Progress for the Nyngle District.
Page-proofs of double-spread with running headlines
Paper the walls, and sets of cigarette-cards
Where pouter-bosomed showgirls still display
The charms that dazzled in the nineteen hundreds.
Through gaping slats
Latticed with sun the ivy tendrils fall
Twining the disused platen thrust away
Under a pall of dust in nineteen-twenty.
Draw up a chair, sit down. Just shift the galleys.
You say you have a notice? There's no one dies
But what we know about it. Births, deaths and marriages,
Council reports, wool prices, river-heights,
The itinerant poem and the classified ads –
They all come homewards to the *Western Star*.
Joe's our type-setter. Meet Joe Burrell. Joe's
A promising lad – and Joe, near forty-seven,
Peers from a tennis-shade and, smiling vaguely,
Completes the headline for the Baptist Social.
The dance, the smoke-oh, and the children's picnic
Down by the river-flats beneath the willows –
They all come homewards and Joe sets them all,
Between the morning and the mid-day schooner.
Oh, *Western Star* that bringest all to fold,
The yarding sales, the champion shorthorn bull,

And Williams' pain-relieving liniment,
When I shall die
Set me up close against my fellow-men,
Cheer that cold column headed 'Deaths' with flowers,
Or mix me up with Births and Marriages;
Surround the tragic statement of my death
With euchre-drives and good-times-had-by-all
That, with these warm concomitants of life
Jostled and cheered, in lower-case italics
I shall go homewards in the *Western Star*.

The Fever

Outside the children play like flames
Over the scorched verandah boards,
The sun burns through the shrinking vine
And Floury Baker calls; his bread
Will not be sold, although all day
He makes his one persistent cry.

My mind like a white butterfly
Moves from the curtain to the sheet,
From sheet to mirror, which returns
All it receives of sky. I seek
The gravity of etchings, lines
As thin as veins, as light as cinders.

You take my temperature and hold
My wrist between your fingers, watch
The seconds pass, attentive, dark,
In city suit, late for your train.
The fitful fancies of my fever
Insist that you have called, a stranger:

Your brief-case is a doctor's bag.
We have not met before, to you
I am a woman sick in bed
Whose children, unattended, play
Outside their shrill, staccato games:
Not yours and mine, of both our making.

If this were so would not my heart
Leap up to recognize with passion
The claim of love for love, to make
Insistent as the shrill cicada
The cry of need, the want of knowing,
One urgent phrase reiterated.

And would you from your unknown life
Of surgery and morning calls,
And home, and wife, and children doubtless,
Would you not meet with recognition
That doomed, entangled, piercing cry?
There is no need for you to answer.

BARBARA GUEST

Green Revolutions

Being drunk upstairs and listening
to voices downstairs. The roll of the sea
sounding calm
                after the voices
and the machinery
                Tibet with Monaco
thrown in for measure

                Distant greens
they appear on walls when one is tired
the dark background greens then the light ones
bringing us closer. As landscape appears
with its fresh basket approaching the car
then relinquishing, going away, telling us
something that is secret, not even whispering,
but indicating as if an ear of corn might be over there
choice and ripe, but neglected.

                The cars go away. The voices
go away. For lunch. At noon.
It's harsh with old Donne in his steeple.
I'm upstairs 'looking at a picture'
like a Bostonian in Florence, 'looking at a picture.'
Now it's green. Now it isn't.

Poem

Disturbing to have a person
So negative beside you
I dreamed last night
The Mississippi Belle rolled over
We were all drowned.

I promise to do better.
Look I have a net here
Filled with trout.

Ain't nothin' like river trout.

GWEN HARWOOD

Hospital Evening

Sunset: the blaze of evening burns
through curtains like a firelit ghost.
Kröte, dreaming of snow, returns
to something horrible on toast

slapped at him by a sulky nurse
whose boyfriend's waiting. Kröte loves
food. Is this food? He finds it worse
than starving, as he cuts and shoves

one nauseating mouthful down.
Kröte has managed to conceal
some brandy in his dressing gown.
He gulps it fast, until the real

sunset's a field of painted light
and his white curtains frame a stage
where he's the hero and must fight
his fever. He begins to rage

fortissimo in German, flings
the empty bottle on the floor;
roars for more brandy, thumps and sings.
Three nurses crackle through the door

and hold him down. He struggles, then
submits to the indignities
nurses inflict, and sleeps again,
dreaming he goes, where the stiff trees

[169]

glitter in silence, hand in hand
with a young child he does not know,
who walking makes no footprint and
no shadow on soft-fallen snow.

In the Bistro

A says 'You're right. He's brilliant but not sound.
This place has the true European fug.'
'Authentic.' B inhales it like a drug.
Tomorrow they will vote, and X be found
wanting. 'We know his kind, my boy. Once bitten . . .
The others will be easy to convince.
Let's try Caucasian whatsit.' (Curried mince.)
It must be twenty years since A has written
a useful word. B begs him to relate
old victories in academic wrangling.
He dreams of his promotion while A pours
a wine not too assertive. His hands wait
lax at his chest. One thinks of the small dangling
forelegs of the flesh-eating dinosaurs.

A Simple Story

A visiting conductor
    when I was seventeen,
took me back to his hotel room
    to cover the music scene.

I'd written a composition.
    Would wonders never cease –
here was a real musician
    prepared to hold my piece.

[170]

He spread my score on the counterpane
   with classic casualness,
and put one hand on the manuscript
   and the other down my dress.

It was hot as hell in The Windsor.
   I said I'd like a drink.
We talked across gin and grapefuit,
   and I heard the ice go clink

as I gazed at the lofty forehead
   of one who led the band,
and guessed at the hoarded sorrows
   no wife could understand.

I dreamed of a soaring passion
   as an egg might dream of flight,
while he read my crude sonata.
   If he'd said, 'That bar's not right,'

or, 'Have you thought of a coda?'
   or, 'Watch that first repeat,'
or, 'Modulate to the dominant,'
   he'd have had me at his feet.

But he shuffled it all together,
   and said, 'That's *lovely*, dear,'
as he put it down on the washstand
   in a way that made it clear

that I was no composer.
   And I being young and vain,
removed my lovely body
   from one who'd scorned my brain.

I swept off like Miss Virtue
  down dusty Roma Street,
and heard the goods trains whistle
  WHO? WHOOOOOO? in aching heat.

DENISE LEVERTOV

Matins

I

The authentic! Shadows of it
sweep past in dreams, one could say imprecisely,
evoking the almost-silent
ripping apart of giant
sheets of cellophane. No.
It thrusts up close. Exactly in dreams
it has you off-guard, you
recognize it before you have time.
For a second before waking
the alarm bell is a red conical hat, it
takes form.

II

The authentic! I said
rising from the toilet seat.
The radiator in rhythmic knockings
spoke of the rising steam.
The authentic, I said
breaking the handle of my hairbrush as I
brushed my hair in
rhythmic strokes: That's it,
that's joy, it's always
a recognition, the known
appearing fully itself, and
more itself than one knew.

III

The new day rises
as heat rises,
knocking in the pipes
with rhythms it seizes for its own
to speak of its invention –
the real, the new-laid
egg whose speckled shell
the poet fondles and must break
if he will be nourished.

IV

A shadow painted where
yes, a shadow must fall.
The cow's breath
not forgotten in the mist, in the
words. Yes,
verisimilitude draws up
heat in us, zest
to follow through,
follow through,
follow
transformations of day
in its turning, in its becoming.

V

Stir the holy grains, set
the bowls on the table and
call the child to eat.

While we eat we think,
as we think an undercurrent
of dream runs through us
faster than thought
towards recognition.

Call the child to eat,
send him off, his mouth
tasting of toothpaste, to go down
into the ground, into a roaring train
and to school.

His cheeks are pink
his black eyes hold his dreams, he has left
forgetting his glasses.

Follow down the stairs at a clatter
to give them to him and save
his clear sight.

Cold air
comes in at the street door.

VI

The authentic! It rolls
just out of reach, beyond
running feet and
stretching fingers, down
the green slope and into
the black waves of the sea.
Speak to me, little horse, beloved,
tell me
how to follow the iron ball,
how to follow through to the country
beneath the waves
to the place where I must kill you and you step out
of your bones and flystrewn meat
tall, smiling, renewed,
formed in your own likeness

VII

Marvelous Truth, confront us
at every turn,
in every guise, iron ball,
egg, dark horse, shadow,
cloud
of breath on the air,

dwell
in our crowded hearts
our steaming bathrooms, kitchens full of
things to be done, the
ordinary streets.

Thrust close your smile
that we know you, terrible joy.

Goethe's Blues

Fantasia on the Trilogie der Leidenschaft

I

The hills stirring under their woven
leaf-nets, sighing, shimmering . . .
High summer.
                    And he with
April anguish tearing him,
heart a young animal, its fur
curly and legs too long.

But he is old. Sere.

                    'O love, O love
                    not unkind,
                    kind,

[176]

my life goes out of me
breath by breath

thinking of your austere
compassion.'

II

Fame tastes 'sweet' to him,
too sweet, and then sour,
and then not at all.

It is not a substance
to taste, it is a box
in which he is kept.

He is a silver
dandelion seed entrapped
in a cube of plexiglass.

III

'Stop the coach! I want to get out
and die!'
   His friends
wonder what he's scribbling,
'furiously', as it is said,
all the way back.
They're doing 80, the freeway's
all theirs.
   'Nature smiles,
and smiles, and
says nothing. And I'm
driving away from the gates of
Paradise.'

Abel's Bride

Woman fears for man, he goes
out alone to his labors. No mirror
nests in his pocket. His face
opens and shuts with his hopes.
His sex hangs unhidden
or rises before him
blind and questing.

She thinks herself
lucky. But sad. When she goes out
she looks in the glass, she remembers
herself. Stones, coal,
the hiss of water upon the kindled
branches – her being
is a cave, there are bones at the hearth.

ELIZABETH BARTLETT

999 Call

He lay on the floor covered in shit,
as he had done all night on his fitted carpet.
It could have been a prison cell or torture room,
but it was in fact the biggest flat in town
as he often boasted, pointing out the Bristol glass,
the original prince of Denmark Hill, brought low.

Stepping round the bed I put my foot in it,
(as the ambulance men said). Kind men, they kept
the joke to themselves, and the policemen said
they'd be independent too (no bloody geriatric ward
for them). I reported how I'd heard him calling me,
the first Sunday visitor checking on people like him.

As he was driven away, the usual voyeurs drifting
off, he said he didn't want to go, and I took off
my soiled sandals and my tights and washed my feet
in his classy bidet, but although I admired
their way of saying 'You've had some trouble
with your motions, sir', I threw my sandals away.

I threw them away as if they had been him, and yet,
he was an arrogant man the neighbours said,
who once sent hats to Buck House and Ascot, in his time,
(those festive hats, those aristocratic faces).
I felt I'd done him dirt, poor chap, and look up
at his louvred windows late at night hoping to see a banner

ELIZABETH, I FORGIVE YOU. NOT YOUR FAULT.

I look, but it is never there.

Charlotte, Her Book

I am Charlotte. I don't say hello
to people and sometimes I bite.
Although I am dead I still jump
out of bed and wake them up at night.

This is my mother. Her hair is blue
and I have drawn her with no eyes
and arms like twigs. I don't do
what I'm told and I tell lies.

This is my father. He has a mouth
under his left ear. I'm fed up
with drawing people, so I scribble
smoke and cover his head right up.

I am a brat kid, fostered out because
my mother is sick in the head,
and I would eat her if I could,
and make her good and dead.

Although I am only four I went away
so soon they hardly knew me,
and stars sprang out of my eyes,
and cold winds blew me.

My mother always says she loves me.
My father says he loves me too.
I love Charlotte. A car ran
over Charlotte. This is her book.

Contre Jour

Contre jour, he said, a photographic phrase,
literally against the day, I suppose.
I'll put a little by, my mother would say,
against the day when we have nothing left.
Limp purse, well-rubbed, false teeth
not quite fitting, second-hand clothes,
knees like nutmeg graters. Whatever happened
to those gentle scented mothers sitting in gardens
under a shady hat, the maid mincing across the grass
with a tray for afternoon tea in early June?
It was never summer for her. It didn't reach
the dank back yard, the airless little rooms,
where the kitchen range brought a flush
to her face as she perpetually bent over it,
cooking, ironing, shifting sooty kettles round,
but never posed for her husband to catch
the tilt of her head against the day,
who never owned a camera anyway.

My inner lens clicks faster, faster,
contre jour, for now her face is fading
as her life recedes. You must have known
that once she minced across the lawn
carrying a loaded tray for mothers
like yours, whose photographs have
frames of silver, like the ones
she polished every week for twelve
pounds per annum and her keep.

PATRICIA BEER

In a Country Museum

This is a strange museum. In one square yard see
A mummified ibis and a postilion's boot.
Grey litter fills the house. For years every dead man
Had some cast-off curious object to donate.

Mindless and slovenly it is, but in one room,
Close to five jars that once held Daffy's Elixir,
Lies something that takes shape. A pallid patchwork quilt
Wrapped in cellophane, is spread on a four-poster.

A card describes the maker, a fourteen-year-old
Servant girl, with no book-learning and no siblings,
Who saved up half-a-crown for the big central piece
Of cloth, and got up at dawn on summer mornings.

This sounds sober and worthy, but the card goes on
To say that, interviewed at eighty, Mrs Brew
Declared it had given her much greater pleasure
Than anything in all her life. If it is true

That to labour on these plodding squares meant more
Than marriage bed, children and a belief in God,
It is the best country marvel in this building
And suitably placed among these bright fields of food.

Middle Age

Middle age at last declares itself
As the time when could-have-been
Is not wishful thinking any more,
Is not, say: I could have been at Oxford
If my parents had been richer
Or if the careers mistress had not thought
Exeter was good enough for me.

It is not misunderstanding either
As when at night in the first year of the war
Bombs could have been thunder
And later on in peace
Thunder could have been bombs.
Sights and sounds are more themselves now.

There have been real alternatives.
They have put on weight and yet faded.

Evening walks go past
Where we could have lived:
The coach-house that the mortgage company
Said had too much charm
And not enough rooms.

Everywhere I look it is the same,
The churchyard or the other side of the bed.
The one who is not lying there
Could have been.

Jane Austen at the Window

When she was young and dancing,
Pregnant women sometimes took
The floor, shamelessly bouncing,
Treating it as a good joke.

In her middle age they loomed
Always larger and larger.
She pitied them. They were doomed
To lose looks, health and figure.

Poor sex objects, animals,
Slack and worn out at thirty.
She pitied with failing pulse.
They lived on to be eighty.

In her last illness she sat
At the window in a caul,
Watching them lurch down the street
Heavy with a funeral.

JANE COOPER

a poem with capital letters

john berryman asked me to write a poem about roosters.
elizabeth bishop, he said, once wrote a poem about roosters.
do your poems use capital letters? he asked. *like god?*
i said. *god no*, he said, *like princeton!* i said,
god preserve me if i ever write a poem about princeton, and i thought,
o john berryman, what has brought me into this company of

                                                                    poets

where the masculine thing to do is use capital letters
and even princeton struts like one of god's betters?

My Young Mother

My young mother, her face narrow
and dark with unresolved wishes
under a hatbrim of the twenties,
stood by my middle-aged bed.

Still as a child pretending sleep
to a grown-up watchful or calling,
I lay in a corner of my dream
staring at the mole above her lip.

Familiar mole! but that girlish look
as if I had nothing to give her –
Eyes blue – brim dark –
calling me from sleep after decades.

[185]

El Sueño de la Razón*

for C. in a mental hospital

Cousin, it's of you I always dream
as I walk these dislocated lawns
or compose a stanza under the Corot trees.

The music of my walking reconciles,
somewhat, the clipped but common ground
with the lost treetops' thunderous heads.

How they are always muttering in the still
afternoon. How they create
their own darkness under hottest sun.

They compose clouds or a sea
so far above us we can scarcely tell
why such a premonition brushes our cheeks.

Yet as I walk I scan
the woods for a girl's white figure
slipping away among the pines' thin shafts.

Hiding, she is hiding, and in your dreams
the poem's cleared spaces
barely hold out

against marching trees, this suddenly Turner sky.
Poor furious girl, our voices sound
alike (your nurse told me), discreet and gentle.

---

*A nightmare etching by Goya is inscribed 'El sueño de la razón
produce monstruos' – 'The dream of reason begets monsters'.

Dispossessions

1 THINGS

Things have their own lives here. The hall chairs
count me as I climb the steps. The piano
is playing at will from behind three potted plants,
while the photograph of the dead girl in the luminescent hat
glows pink since the lamp lighted itself at four.

We are very humane here. Of course people
go off course sometimes, radio to the outside world
only through typewriter noise or the bathwater running.
And then the empty glasses, the books on health food left
around . . .
But the things have been here longer then we have.

And the trees are older even than furniture.
They were here to witness the original drownings
(because I always think the children drowned, no matter what
you say).
Last night a voice called me from outside my door.
It was no one's voice, perhaps it came from the umbrella stand.

2 SOUVENIRS

Anyway we are always waking
in bedrooms of the dead, smelling
musk of their winter jackets, tracking
prints of their heels across our blurred carpets.

So why hang onto a particular postcard?
If a child's lock of hair brings back
the look of that child, shall I
nevertheless not let it blow away?

Houses, houses, we lodge in such husks!
inhabit such promises, seeking the unborn
in a worn-out photograph, hoping to break free
even of our violent and faithful lives.

3 INHERITANCES*

Malte Laurids, peevish: *And one has
nothing and nobody, travels about the world
with a few clothes and a satchel of books. What sort of life
is it? without a house, without
inheritances* (the Chamberlain's eyeglasses, say,
in a glass case?), *without
dogs –*

Yet he wrote the Chamberlain's death, explaining:
*I have taken action against fear, I
have sat all night and written.*

And: *Still it is not enough
to have memories, they
must turn to blood inside you.*

---

*Quoted virtually in its entirety from Rilke's *The Notebooks of Malte Laurids
Brigge*, translated by M. D. Herter Norton.

LAURIS EDMOND

A Difficult Adjustment

It takes time, and there are setbacks;
on Monday, now, you were all ennui
and malice; but this morning I am
pleased with my handiwork: your
stick figure moves, your two eyes
are large and dark enough, your
expression is conveniently mild.
You have begun to disagree with me,
but weakly, so that I can easily prove
you wrong. In fact you are entirely
satisfactory.

    I suppose, really, you are
dead. But someone silently lies down
with me at night and shows a soothing
tenderness. I have killed the pain
of bone and flesh; I suffer no laughter
now, nor hear the sound of troubled
voices speaking in the dark.

The Sums

Somewhere you are always going home;
some shred of the rag of events
is for ever being torn off and kept
in an inside pocket or creased satchel
like the crayon drawing, blurred now,
you frowned over once in a desk

– it's kept for the moment when you go
mooching along the verandah and through
the back door, brass-handled, always ajar,
to where the floured apron stands monumental
above veined legs in a cloud of savoury steam,
mince, onions, the smell of childhood's Julys;

there again you are quick-flounced and shrill
shrieking on a high stool the answers
to sums – multiplication, addition, subtraction,
all the mysteries known as 'Mental', alchemy
that could transmute 48 + 17 (when you got it,
yelling) to a burst of fire in the blood –

it is still there, still finding its
incorruptible, useless answers,
your life's ruined verandah, the apron,
the disfigured legs that with a stolid
magnificence used to hold up the world.

MAXINE KUMIN

In the Root Cellar

The parsnips, those rabbis
have braided their beards together
to examine the text. The word
that engrosses them is: February.

To be a green tomato
wrapped in the Sunday book section
is to know nothing. Meanwhile
the wet worm eats his way outward.

These cabbages, these clean keepers
in truth are
a row of impacted stillbirths.
One by one we deliver them.

The apples are easy abutters
a basket of pulltoys and smiles.
Still, they infect one another
like children exchanging the measles.

O potato, a wink of
daylight and you're up with
ten tentative erections.
How they deplete you!

Dusty blue wart hogs, the squash
squat for a thump and a tuning.
If we could iron them out
they'd be patient blue mandolins.

The beets wait wearing their birthmarks.
They will be wheeled into the amphitheater.
Even before the scrub-up, the scalpel,
they bleed a little.

I am perfect, breathes the onion.
I am God's first circle
the tulip that slept in His navel.
Bite me and be born.

The Retrieval System

It begins with my dog, now dead, who all his long life
carried about in his head the brown eyes of my father,
keen, loving, accepting, sorrowful, whatever;
they were Daddy's all right, handed on, except
for their phosphorescent gleam tunneling the night
which I have to concede was a separate gift.

Uncannily when I'm alone these features
come up to link my lost people
with the patient domestic beasts of my life. For example,
the wethered goat who runs free in pasture and stable
with his flecked, agate eyes and his minus-sign pupils
blats in the tiny voice of my former piano teacher

whose bones beat time in my dreams and whose terrible breath
soured *Country Gardens*, *Humoresque*, and unplayable Bach.
My elderly aunts, wearing the heads of willful
intelligent ponies, stand at the fence begging apples.
The sister who died at three has my cat's faint chin,
my cat's inscrutable squint, and cried catlike in pain.

I remember the funeral. *The Lord is my shepherd*,
we said. I don't want to brood. Fact: it is people who fade,
it is animals that retrieve them. A boy
I loved once keeps coming back as my yearling colt,
cocksure at the gallop, racing his shadow
for the hell of it. He runs merely to be.
A boy who was lost in the war thirty years ago
and buried at sea.

Here, it's forty degrees and raining. The weatherman
who looks like my resident owl, the one who goes out and in
by the open haymow, appears on the TV screen.
With his heart-shaped face, he is also my late dentist's double,
donnish, bifocaled, kind. Going a little gray,
advising this wisdom tooth will have to come out someday,
meanwhile filling it as a favor. Another save.
It outlasted him. The forecast is nothing but trouble.
It will snow fiercely enough to fill all these open graves.

The Excrement Poem

It is done by us all, as God disposes, from
the least cast of worm to what must have been
in the case of the brontosaur, say, spoor
of considerable heft, something awesome.

We eat, we evacuate, survivors that we are.
I think these things each morning with shovel
and rake, drawing the risen brown buns
toward me, fresh from the horse oven, as it were,

or culling the alfalfa-green ones, expelled
in a state of ooze, through the sawdust bed
to take a serviceable form, as putty does,
so as to lift out entire from the stall.

[193]

And wheeling to it, storming up the slope,
I think of the angle of repose the manure
pile assumes, how sparrows come to pick
the redelivered grain, how inky-cap

coprinus mushrooms spring up in a downpour.
I think of what drops from us and must then
be moved to make way for the next and next.
However much we stain the world, spatter

it with our leavings, make stenches, defile
the great formal oceans with what leaks down,
trundling off today's last barrowful,
I honor shit for saying: We go on.

ELIZABETH JENNINGS

One Flesh

Lying apart now, each in a separate bed,
He with a book, keeping the light on late,
She like a girl dreaming of childhood,
All men elsewhere – it is as if they wait
Some new event: the book he holds unread,
Her eyes fixed on the shadows overhead.

Tossed up like flotsam from a former passion,
How cool they lie. They hardly ever touch,
Or if they do it is like a confession
Of having little feeling – or too much.
Chastity faces them, a destination
For which their whole lives were a preparation.

Strangely apart, yet strangely close together,
Silence between them like a thread to hold
And not wind in. And time itself's a feather
Touching them gently. Do they know they're old,
These two who are my father and my mother
Whose fire from which I came, has now grown cold?

Fragment for the Dark

Let it not come near me, let it not
Fold round or over me. One weak hand
Clutches a foot of air, asks the brisk buds
To suffer grey winds, spear through
Fog I feel in me. Give me the magic
To see grounded starlings, their polish
As this threat of all-day night. Mind, mind
In me, make thoughts candles to light me
Out of the furthest reach of possible nights.
Lantern me, stars, if I look up through wet hands,
Show assurance in blurred shining. I have
Put every light in the house on.
May their filaments last till true morning.

ANNE SZUMIGALSKI

Want of þ want of ð

stitch in the side
thorn in the mouth
between tongue and teeth
carmen the glowing carmine of the rose

what happens
going home after the dance?
it's thrown aside
droops its red head
on the gravel of the road
that leads away from the factory

the flower signifies a man at arms
his ceremonial strut
or could be a guerilla lying
at ambush in the long ditch grass

these fall, both cast in the sand
of someone else's glory
while each word held above
the shifting air thins
to less than a syllable

an unvoiced thorn
anther anthem
the easter church
swirls with spring pollen
two young sisters lift their arms
their hands deck the windowsills
with primrose and sallow
catkin exhaling that heady

stink of sap   a veil
for each newly-confirmed head
here follows in quires the anthem
rising like smoke
from their virginal fires

mother has clothed them in neat frocks
with wide quaker collars
before summer brings the rose
whose red dye stains the lips
its thorns like cigarettes

what have we left to us
at our age? one sister writes
you wanted to judge
I wanted to pronounce
sentences   neither of us
kept to our maiden calling

(ah the red-stained tongue
between nicotine teeth)

edh edh something always missing
from the mouth   laziness
at the foundry
loss at the font
a blank in the vocabulary
of desire *loth love that tethers thee*
it's a gap grin

and so we lisp on to the grave
sons and daughters follow
the book on the lectern closes
the purple cloth pulled over
the ancient face now fades
the primrose, withers the rose
what was it that we suffered
that we shared?
lack of a letter for an apidental sound?

this sharp and sudden pain in the side
the compositor's error

In the Heat of the Morning

albert is haranguing his mother about his name
complaining as usual about how unsuitable it is
she knows that then why for godsake? she tells
how once there was a royal prince but when he
came to be king he was suddenly george like the
rest

you don't know how embarrassing it is in class
among the marks and olivers even james is a king
and a saint at our school saint simeon stylites has
it over all the rest *saint simeon's secondary school*
he yells these words at her over and over this
argument is finished call yourself al or bertie or
whatever you want I'm going in to take a bath
and she drops her trowel and coarse leather gloves
into the low basket she's using for weeds

albert is into wild plants and doesn't call any-
thing a weed it is his belief that darnel and alex-
anders will inherit the earth from his mother's
damask roses which have been tame since the
time of the persians xerxes would have been a
fair name or xenophon good thing I'm not a girl
she might have named me rose tokio rose I love
you I'll always dream of you some of those japa-
nese cultivars have poison hips pip hooray but
then consider *rosa centifolia muscosa* its crowded
petals and many weak thorns even the buds are
edible

at the funeral he insists they are to call him mr
carew now that he's head of the family what
family counters the reverend you are the last of
the bunch albert and anyway you are fifteen and
a ward of the court my mother spoke of a half-
sister replies mr carew with dignity he is led to an
overgrown part of the churchyard here lies rozalia
daughter of euphemia you women he accuses
them in his heart have gone before me and left
me alone in this social blaze while you rest in your
cool tombs

MOLLY HOLDEN

Seaman, 1941

This was not to be expected.

Waves, wind, and tide brought him again
to Barra. Clinging to driftwood many hours
the night before, he had not recognized
the current far offshore his own nor
known he drifted home. He gave up, anyway,
some time before the smell of land reached out
or dawn outlined the morning gulls.

                             They found him
on the white sand southward of the ness,
not long enough in the sea to be
disfigured, cheek sideways as in sleep,
old men who had fished with his father
and grandfather and knew him at once,
before they even turned him on his back, by the set
of the dead shoulders, and were shocked.

This was not to be expected.

His mother, with hot eyes, preparing the parlour
for his corpse, would have preferred, she thought,
to have been told by telegram rather
than so to know that convoy, ship, and son
had only been a hundred miles north-west
of home when the torpedoes struck.
She could have gone on thinking that
he'd had no chance; but to die offshore,
in Hebridean tides, as if he'd stayed
a fisherman for life and never gone to war
was not to be expected.

CONNIE BENSLEY

Desires

Newly shaven, your eyes only slightly bloodshot,
Your rat-trap mouth smiling up at the corners,
You remind me of the Head Girl
I used to be in love with.

It's something about your sporty build,
The way you seem to be counting the people in the café
With a view to lining them up in teams.

It's quite set me in the mood for the evening,
And I follow you alertly through the door,
Hoping you'll turn and snap at me
To pick my feet up, and not to slouch.

Charity

Trouble has done her good,
Trouble has stopped her trivializing everything,
Giggling too much,
Glittering after other people's husbands.

Trouble has made her think;
Taken her down a peg,
Knocked the stuffing out of her.
Trouble has toned down the vulgarity.

Under the bruises she looks more deserving:
Someone you'd be glad to throw a rope to,
Somewhere to send your old blouses,
Or those wormy little windfalls.

FREDA DOWNIE

Great-grandfather

Great-grandfather would sit in the back parlour
For hours listening to the gramophone.
I have no photograph of him doing this,
So the picture I see of him sitting alone

With his head inclined towards the trumpeting
Green lily is colourful and unfaded.
The handkerchief, with which he blots the tears
Schubert serenades from him, is distinctly red

And the gramophone's tin horn grows steadily
More greenly lily-like and rare,
Grows into antiquity – and soon will be found
Surviving only behind glass in conditioned air.

Great-grandfather knows nothing of this, but
Such an instrument will be treasured as though
It were a silver trumpet once discovered
Lying in the tomb of some young Egyptian Pharaoh;

And only on certain occasions will it be taken
From its case and played with careful ceremony –
When thinnest sound will summon the ready armies
Of imagination to salute the music lovers of history.

And great-grandfather will be one of those.

Her Garden

My grandmother grew tiny grapes and tiger-lilies,
But there is no sentimental cut to her garden
Through a fat album or remembered lane;
Only interior voyages made on London ferries

Paddling the Thames' wicked brew to Silvertown,
Where regular as boot boys, the factories
Blacked her house every day, obscured the skies
And the town's sweet name at the railway station.

Between ships parked at the end of the road
And factory gates, she kept her home against soot,
Kept her garden colours in spite of it –
Five square feet of bitterness in a paved yard

Turned to the silent flowering of her will,
Loaded with dusty beauty and natural odours,
Cinnamon lilies, and the vine roots hanging grapes,
Sour as social justice, on the wash-house wall.

Starlight

Three kings embark on a long journey
Under the dry acres of the moon,
Whose light is well disposed,
But of no special significance.

It is the nailhead light
Of one sparky planet
That draws them on –
Although at times,
One king thinks the star
Has the look of crayon
Drawn on dark paper;
While another thinks it
Looks no more than a sliver
Of silver pasted on indigo;
And the third king, observing
A certain unsteadiness,
Thinks the heavenly guide
Trembles on its cotton thread.

Miss Grant

Oneself Miss Grant,
Sufficient in the white walls
Around the necessary furniture
And one dog to talk to by the fire.

Resigned to the baker's call,
The plopped frog on the parlour floor
For excitement, framed relations
And receded nephews in naval attire.

One Bessie cow to pursue
In the deep drenched garden endless
To the dripping honeysuckle
And boulders on the lip of the loch.

No distraction or running water,
But the mountainous moving picture,
The pouring stream and tile-hung
Curtain of rain before the sun's lick.

One life to finish
According to the windowsill's book
In Gaelic, as big as a tombstone
And appropriately black.

U. A. FANTHORPE

Not My Best Side

I

Not my best side, I'm afraid.
The artist didn't give me a chance to
Pose properly, and as you can see,
Poor chap, he had this obsession with
Triangles, so he left off two of my
Feet. I didn't comment at the time
(What, after all, are two feet
To a monster?) but afterwards
I was sorry for the bad publicity.
Why, I said to myself, should my conqueror
Be so ostentatiously beardless, and ride
A horse with a deformed neck and square hoofs?
Why should my victim be so
Unattractive as to be inedible,
And why should she have me literally
On a string? I don't mind dying
Ritually, since I always rise again,
But I should have liked a little more blood
To show they were taking me seriously.

II

It's hard for a girl to be sure if
She wants to be rescued. I mean, I quite
Took to the dragon. It's nice to be
Liked, if you know what I mean. He was
So nicely physical, with his claws
And lovely green skin, and that sexy tail,
And the way he looked at me,

He made me feel he was all ready to
Eat me. And any girl enjoys that.
So when this boy turned up, wearing machinery,
On a really *dangerous* horse, to be honest,
I didn't much fancy him. I mean,
What was he like underneath the hardware?
He might have acne, blackheads or even
Bad breath for all I could tell, but the dragon –
Well, you could see all his equipment
At a glance. Still, what could I do?
The dragon got himself beaten by the boy,
And a girl's got to think of her future.

III

I have diplomas in Dragon
Management and Virgin Reclamation.
My horse is the latest model, with
Automatic transmission and built-in
Obsolescence. My spear is custom-built,
And my prototype armour
Still on the secret list. You can't
Do better than me at the moment.
I'm qualified and equipped to the
Eyebrow. So why be difficult?
Don't you want to be killed and/or rescued
In the most contemporary way? Don't
You want to carry out the roles
That sociology and myth have designed for you?
Don't you realize that, by being choosy,
You are endangering job-prospects
In the spear- and horse-building industries?
What, in any case, does it matter what
You want? You're in my way.

At the Ferry

Laconic as anglers and, like them, submissive,
The grey-faced loiterers on the bank,
Charon, of your river.

They are waiting their turn. Nothing we do
Distracts them much. It was you, Charon, I saw,
Refracted in a woman's eyes.

Patient, she sat in a wheelchair,
In an X-ray department, waiting for someone
To do something to her,

Given a magazine, folded back
At the problem page: *What should I do*
About my husband's impotence?

Is a registry office marriage
Second-best? I suffer from a worrying
Discharge from my vagina.

In her hands she held the thing obediently;
Obediently moved her eyes in the direction
Of the problems of the restless living.

But her mind deferred to another dimension.
Outward bound, tenderly inattentive, she was waiting,
Charon, for you.

And the nineteen-stone strong man, felled
By his spawning brain, lying still to the sound
Of the DJ's brisk chirrup;

He wasn't listening, either. He was on the lookout
For the flurry of water as your craft
Comes about in the current.

I saw you once, boatman, lean by your punt-pole
On an Oxford river, in the dubious light
Between willow and water,

Where I had been young and lonely, being
Now loved, and older; saw you in the tender, reflective
Gaze of the living

Looking down at me, deliberate,
And strange in the half-light, saying nothing,
Claiming me, Charon, for life.

Resuscitation Team

Arrives like a jinn, instantly,
Equipped with beards, white coats, its own smell,
And armfuls of metal and rubber.

Deploys promptly round the quiet bed
With horseplay and howls of laughter.
We, who are used to life, are surprised

At this larky resurrection. Runs
Through its box of tricks, prick, poke and biff,
While we watch, amazed. The indifferent patient

Is not amused, but carries little weight,
Being stripped and fumbled
By so many rugger-players. My first corpse,

If she is a corpse, lies there showing
Too much breast and leg. The team
Rowdily throws up the sponge, demands soap and water,

Leaves at the double. One of us,
Uncertainly, rearranges the night-dress.
Is it professional to observe the proprieties

Now of her who leaves privately
Wheeled past closed doors, her face
Still in the rictus of victory?

Father in the Railway Buffet

What are you doing here, ghost, among these urns,
These film-wrapped sandwiches and help-yourself biscuits,
Upright and grand, with your stick, hat and gloves,
Your breath of eau-de-cologne?

What have you to say to these head-scarfed tea-ladies,
For whom your expensive vowels are exotic as Japan?
Stay, ghost, in your proper haunts, the clubland smoke-rooms,
Where you know the waiters by name.

You have no place among these damp and nameless.
Why do you walk here? *I came to say goodbye.*
You were ashamed of me for being different.
It didn't matter.

You who never even learned to queue?

ADRIENNE RICH

Aunt Jennifer's Tigers

Aunt Jennifer's tigers prance across a screen,
Bright topaz denizens of a world of green.
They do not fear the men beneath the tree;
They pace in sleek chivalric certainty.

Aunt Jennifer's fingers fluttering through her wool
Find even the ivory needle hard to pull.
The massive weight of Uncle's wedding band
Sits heavily upon Aunt Jennifer's hand.

When Aunt is dead, her terrified hands will lie
Still ringed with ordeals she was mastered by.
The tigers in the panel that she made
Will go on prancing, proud and unafraid.

Focus

for Bert Dreyfus

Obscurity has its tale to tell.
Like the figure on the studio-bed in the corner,

out of range, smoking, watching and waiting.
Sun pours through the skylight onto the worktable

making of a jar of pencils, a typewriter keyboard
more than they were. Veridical light . . .

Earth budges. Now an empty coffee-cup,
a whetstone, a handkerchief, take on

their sacramental clarity, fixed by the wand
of light as the thinker thinks to fix them in the mind.

O secret in the core of the whetstone, in the five
pencils splayed out like fingers of a hand!

The mind's passion is all for singling out.
Obscurity has another tale to tell.

Snapshots of a Daughter-in-Law

1

You, once a belle in Shreveport,
with henna-colored hair, skin like a peachbud,
still have your dresses copied from that time,
and play a Chopin prelude
called by Cortot: *'Delicious recollections*
float like perfume through the memory.'

Your mind now, moldering like wedding-cake,
heavy with useless experience, rich
with suspicion, rumor, fantasy,
crumbling to pieces under the knife-edge
of mere fact. In the prime of your life.

Nervy, glowering, your daughter
wipes the teaspoons, grows another way.

2

Banging the coffee-pot into the sink
she hears the angels chiding, and looks out
past the raked gardens to the sloppy sky.
Only a week since They said: *Have no patience.*

The next time it was: *Be insatiable*.
Then: *Save yourself; others you cannot save*.
Sometimes she's let the tapstream scald her arm,
a match burn to her thumbnail,

or held her hand above the kettle's snout
right in the woolly steam. They are probably angels,
since nothing hurts her any more, except
each morning's grit blowing into her eyes.

3

A thinking woman sleeps with monsters.
The beak that grips her, she becomes. And Nature,
that sprung-lidded, still commodious
steamer-trunk of *tempora* and *mores*
gets stuffed with it all: the mildewed orange-flowers,
the female pills, the terrible breasts
of Boadicea beneath flat foxes' heads and orchids.

Two handsome women, gripped in argument,
each proud, acute, subtle, I hear scream
across the cut glass and majolica
like Furies cornered from their prey:
The argument *ad feminam*, all the old knives
that have rusted in my back, I drive in yours,
ma semblable, ma soeur!

4

Knowing themselves too well in one another:
their gifts no pure fruition, but a thorn,
the prick filed sharp against a hint of scorn . . .
Reading while waiting
for the iron to heat,
writing, *My Life had stood – a Loaded Gun –*

in that Amherst pantry while the jellies boil and scum,
or, more often,
iron-eyed and beaked and purposed as a bird,
dusting everything on the whatnot every day of life.

5

Dulce ridens, dulce loquens
she shaves her legs until they gleam
like petrified mammoth-tusk.

6

When to her lute Corinna sings
neither words nor music are her own;
only the long hair dipping
over her cheek, only the song
of silk against her knees
and these
adjusted in reflections of an eye.

Poised, trembling and unsatisfied, before
an unlocked door, that cage of cages,
tell us, you bird, you tragical machine –
is this *fertilisante douleur*? Pinned down
by love, for you the only natural action,
are you edged more keen
to prise the secrets of the vault? has Nature shown
her household books to you, daughter-in-law,
that her sons never saw?

7

'To have in this uncertain world some stay
which cannot be undermined, is
of the utmost consequence.'
                              Thus wrote
a woman, partly brave and partly good,

[216]

who fought with what she partly understood.
Few men about her would or could do more,
hence she was labeled harpy, shrew and whore.

8

'You all die at fifteen,' said Diderot,
and turn part legend, part convention.
Still, eyes inaccurately dream
behind closed windows blankening with steam.
Deliciously, all that we might have been,
all that we were – fire, tears,
wit, taste, martyred ambition –
stirs like the memory of refused adultery
the drained and flagging bosom of our middle years.

9

Not that it is done well, but
that it is done at all? Yes, think
of the odds! or shrug them off forever.
This luxury of the precocious child,
Time's precious chronic invalid, –
would we, darlings, resign it if we could?
Our blight has been our sinecure:
mere talent was enough for us –
glitter in fragments and rough drafts.

Sigh no more, ladies.
                    Time is male
and in his cups drink to the fair.
Bemused by gallantry, we hear
our mediocrities over-praised,
indolence read as abnegation,

slattern thought styled intuition,
every lapse forgiven, our crime
only to cast too bold a shadow
or smash the mold straight off.

For that, solitary confinement,
tear gas, attrition shelling.
Few applicants for that honor.

10

Well,
she's long about her coming, who must be
more merciless to herself than history.
Her mind full to the wind, I see her plunge
breasted and glancing through the currents,
taking the light upon her
at least as beautiful as any boy
or helicopter,
poised, still coming,
her fine blades making the air wince

but her cargo
no promise then:
delivered
palpable
ours.

Planetarium

*Thinking of Caroline Herschel, 1750–1848, astronomer, sister of
William; and others*

A woman in the shape of a monster
a monster in the shape of a woman
the skies are full of them

a woman   'in the snow
among the Clocks and instruments
or measuring the ground with poles'

in her 98 years to discover
8 comets

she whom the moon ruled
like us
levitating into the night sky
riding the polished lenses

Galaxies of women, there
doing penance for impetuousness
ribs chilled
in those spaces   of the mind

An eye,
          'virile, precise and absolutely certain'
          from the mad webs of Uranusborg

                              encountering the NOVA

every impulse of light exploding
from the core
as life flies out of us
          Tycho whispering at last
          'Let me not seem to have lived in vain'

[219]

What we see, we see
and seeing is changing

the light that shrivels a mountain
and leaves a man alive

Heartbeat of the pulsar
heart sweating through my body

The radio impulse
pouring in from Taurus

      I am bombarded yet   I stand

I have been standing all my life in the
direct path of a battery of signals
the most accurately transmitted most
untranslateable language in the universe
I am a galactic cloud so deep   so invo-
luted that a light wave could take 15
years to travel through me   And has
taken   I am an instrument in the shape
of a woman trying to translate pulsations
into images   for the relief of the body
and the reconstruction of the mind.

from Shooting Script

9
NEWSREEL

This would not be the war we fought in. See, the foliage is heavier, there were no hills of that size there.

But I find it impossible not to look for actual persons known to me and not seen since; impossible not to look for myself.

The scenery angers me, I know there is something wrong, the sun
is too high, the grass too trampled, the peasants' faces too broad,
and the main square of the capital had no arcades like those.

Yet the dead look right, and the roofs of the huts, and the crashed
fuselage burning among the ferns.

But this is not the war I came to see, buying my ticket, stumbling
through the darkness, finding my place among the sleepers and
masturbators in the dark.

I thought of seeing the General who cursed us, whose name they
gave to an expressway; I wanted to see the faces of the dead
when they were living.

Once I know they filmed us, back at the camp behind the lines,
taking showers under the trees and showing pictures of our girls.

Somewhere there is a film of the war we fought in, and it must
contain the flares, the souvenirs, the shadows of the netted brush
the standing in line of the innocent, the hills that were not of this
size.

Somewhere my body goes taut under the deluge, somewhere I
am naked behind the lines, washing my body in the water of that
war.

Someone has that war stored up in metal canisters, a memory he
cannot use, somewhere my innocence is proven with my guilt,
but this would not be the war I fought in.

11

The mare's skeleton in the clearing: another sign of life.

When you pull the embedded bones up from the soil, the flies
collect again.

[221]

The pelvis, the open archway, staring at me like an eye.

In the desert these bones would be burnt white; a green bloom grows on them in the woods.

Did she break her leg or die of poison?

What was it like when the scavengers came?

So many questions unanswered, yet the statement is here and clear.

With what joy you handled the skull, set back the teeth spilt in the grass, hinged back the jaw on the jaw.

With what joy we left the woods, swinging our sticks, miming the speech of noble savages, of the fathers of our country, bursting into the full sun of the uncut field.

14

Whatever it was: the grains of the glacier caked in the boot-cleats; ashes spilled on white formica.

The death-col viewed through power-glasses; the cube of ice melting on stainless steel.

Whatever it was, the image that stopped you, the one on which you came to grief, projecting it over & over on empty walls.

Now to give up the temptations of the projector; to see instead the web of cracks filtering across the plaster.

To read there the map of the future, the roads radiating from the initial split, the filaments thrown out from that impasse.

To reread the instructions on your palm; to find there how the lifeline, broken, keeps its direction.

To read the etched rays of the bullet-hole left years ago in the glass; to know in every distortion of the light what fracture is.

To put the prism in your pocket, the thin glass lens, the map of the inner city, the little book with gridded pages.

To pull yourself up by your own roots; to eat the last meal in your old neighborhood.

Waking in the Dark

1

The thing that arrests me is
  how we are composed of molecules

  (he showed me the figure in the paving stones)

  arranged without our knowledge and consent

    like the wirephoto composed
    of millions of dots
    in which the man from Bangladesh
    walks starving
          on the front page
          knowing nothing about it

    which is his presence for the world

2

We were standing in line outside of something
two by two, or alone in pairs, or simply alone,
looking into windows full of scissors,
windows full of shoes. The street was closing,
the city was closing, would we be the lucky ones
to make it? They were showing
in a glass case, the Man Without A Country.
We held up our passports in his face, we wept for him.

They are dumping animal blood into the sea.
to bring up the sharks. Sometimes every
aperture of my body
leaks blood. I don't know whether
to pretend that this is natural.
Is there a law about this, a law of nature?
You worship the blood
you call it hysterical bleeding
you want to drink it like milk
you dip your finger into it and write
you faint at the smell of it
you dream of dumping me into the sea.

3

The tragedy of sex
lies around us, a woodlot
the axes are sharpened for.
The old shelters and huts
stare through the clearing with a certain resolution
– the hermit's cabin, the hunters' shack –
scenes of masturbation
and dirty jokes.
A man's world. But finished.
They themselves have sold it to the machines.
I walk the unconscious forest,

[224]

a woman dressed in old army fatigues
that have shrunk to fit her, I am lost
at moments, I feel dazed
by the sun pawing between the trees,
cold in the bog and lichen of the thicket.
Nothing will save this. I am alone,
kicking the last rotting logs
with their strange smell of life, not death,
wondering what on earth it all might have become.

4

Clarity,
     spray

blinding and purging

spears of sun striking the water

the bodies riding the air

like gliders

the bodies in slow motion

falling
into the pool
at the Berlin Olympics

control; loss of control

the bodies rising
arching back to the tower
time reeling backward

clarity of open air
before the dark chambers
with the shower-heads

the bodies falling again
freely

                faster than light
the water opening
like air
like realization

A woman made this film
against

the law
of gravity

5

All night dreaming of a body
space weighs on differently from mine
We are making love in the street
the traffic flows off from us
pouring back like a sheet
the asphalt stirs with tenderness
there is no dismay
we move together like underwater plants

Over and over, starting to wake
I dive back to discover you
still whispering, *touch me*, we go on
streaming through the slow
citylight forest ocean
stirring our body hair

But this is the saying of a dream
on waking
I wish there were somewhere
actual we could stand
handing the power-glasses back and forth
looking at the earth, the wildwood
where the split began

ELAINE FEINSTEIN

Lais

Lais, courtesan of Corinth, why has
Holbein given you so mild a face,
and why now does your gentle hand lie open
beside those golden coins you do not take?

Sad mother and serious, your service
must be in some way most benevolent,
a holy trimmer in this Protestant city:
you cannot hide the evidence of grace.

Patience

In water nothing is mean. The fugitive
enters the river, she is washed free;
her thoughts unravel like weeds of
green silk: she moves downstream
as easily as any cold-water creature

can swim between furred stones, brown
fronds, boots and tins the river holds equally.
The trees hiss overhead. She feels their shadows.
She imagines herself clean as a fish,
evasive, solitary, dumb. Her prayer:
to make peace with her own monstrous nature.

JENNY JOSEPH

Warning

When I am an old woman I shall wear purple
With a red hat which doesn't go, and doesn't suit me.
And I shall spend my pension on brandy and summer gloves
And satin sandals, and say we've no money for butter.
I shall sit down on the pavement when I'm tired
And gobble up samples in shops and press alarm bells
And run my stick along the public railings
And make up for the sobriety of my youth.
I shall go out in my slippers in the rain
And pick the flowers in other people's gardens
And learn to spit.

You can wear terrible shirts and grow more fat
And eat three pounds of sausages at a go
Or only bread and pickle for a week
And hoard pens and pencils and beermats and things in boxes.

But now we must have clothes that keep us dry
And pay our rent and not swear in the street
And set a good example for the children.
We must have friends to dinner and read the papers.

But maybe I ought to practise a little now?
So people who know me are not too shocked and surprised
When suddenly I am old, and start to wear purple.

SYLVIA PLATH

Spinster

Now this particular girl
During a ceremonious April walk
With her latest suitor
Found herself, of a sudden, intolerably struck
By the birds' irregular babel
And the leaves' litter.

By this tumult afflicted, she
Observed her lover's gestures unbalance the air,
His gait stray uneven
Through a rank wilderness of fern and flower.
She judged petals in disarray,
The whole season, sloven.

How she longed for winter then! –
Scrupulously austere in its order
Of white and black
Ice and rock, each sentiment within border,
And heart's frosty discipline
Exact as a snowflake.

But here – a burgeoning
Unruly enough to pitch her five queenly wits
Into vulgar motley –
A treason not to be borne. Let idiots
Reel giddy in bedlam spring:
She withdrew neatly.

And round her house she set
Such a barricade of barb and check
Against mutinous weather
As no mere insurgent man could hope to break
With curse, fist, threat
Or love, either.

The Manor Garden

The fountains are dry and the roses over.
Incense of death. Your day approaches.
The pears fatten like little buddhas.
A blue mist is dragging the lake.

You move through the era of fishes,
The smug centuries of the pig –
Head, toe and finger
Come clear of the shadow. History

Nourishes these broken flutings,
These crowns of acanthus,
And the crow settles her garments.
You inherit white heather, a bee's wing,

Two suicides, the family wolves,
Hours of blankness. Some hard stars
Already yellow the heavens.
The spider on its own string

Crosses the lake. The worms
Quit their usual habitations.
The small birds converge, converge
With their gifts to a difficult borning.

The Colossus

I shall never get you put together entirely,
Pieced, glued, and properly jointed.
Mule-bray, pig-grunt and bawdy cackles
Proceed from your great lips.
It's worse than a barnyard.

Perhaps you consider yourself an oracle,
Mouthpiece of the dead, or of some god or other.
Thirty years now I have laboured
To dredge the silt from your throat.
I am none the wiser.

Scaling little ladders with gluepots and pails of lysol
I crawl like an ant in mourning
Over the weedy acres of your brow
To mend the immense skull-plates and clear
The bald, white tumuli of your eyes.

A blue sky out of the Oresteia
Arches above us. O father, all by yourself
You are pithy and historical as the Roman Forum.
I open my lunch on a hill of black cypress.
Your fluted bones and acanthine hair are littered

In their old anarchy to the horizon-line.
It would take more than a lightning-stroke
To create such a ruin.
Nights, I squat in the cornucopia
Of your left ear, out of the wind,

Counting the red stars and those of plum-colour.
The sum rises under the pillar of your tongue.
My hours are married to shadow.
No longer do I listen for the scrape of a keel
On the blank stones of the landing.

Mushrooms

Overnight, very
Whitely, discreetly,
Very quietly

Our toes, our noses
Take hold on the loam,
Acquire the air.

Nobody sees us,
Stops us, betrays us;
The small grains make room.

Soft fists insist on
Heaving the needles,
The leafy bedding,

Even the paving.
Our hammers, our rams,
Earless and eyeless,

Perfectly voiceless,
Widen the crannies,
Shoulder through holes. We

Diet on water,
On crumbs of shadow,
Bland-mannered, asking

Little or nothing.
So many of us!
So many of us!

We are shelves, we are
Tables, we are meek,
We are edible,

Nudgers and shovers
In spite of ourselves.
Our kind multiplies:

We shall by morning
Inherit the earth.
Our foot's in the door.

You're

Clownlike, happiest on your hands,
Feet to the stars, and moon-skulled,
Gilled like a fish. A common-sense
Thumbs-down on the dodo's mode.
Wrapped up in yourself like a spool,
Trawling your dark as owls do.
Mute as a turnip from the Fourth
Of July to All Fools' Day,
O high-riser, my little loaf.

[234]

Vague as fog and looked for like mail.
Farther off than Australia.
Bent-backed Atlas, our travelled prawn.
Snug as a bud and at home
Like a sprat in a pickle jug.
A creel of eels, all ripples.
Jumpy as a Mexican bean.
Right, like a well-done sum.
A clean slate, with your own face on.

The Moon and the Yew Tree

This is the light of the mind, cold and planetary.
The trees of the mind are black. The light is blue.
The grasses unload their griefs on my feet as if I were God,
Prickling my ankles and murmuring of their humility.
Fumy, spiritous mists inhabit this place
Separated from my house by a row of headstones.
I simply cannot see where there is to get to.

The moon is no door. It is a face in its own right,
White as a knuckle and terribly upset.
It drags the sea after it like a dark crime; it is quiet
With the O-gape of complete despair. I live here.
Twice on Sunday, the bells startle the sky –
Eight great tongues affirming the Resurrection.
At the end, they soberly bong out their names.

The yew tree points up. It has a Gothic shape.
The eyes lift after it and find the moon.
The moon is my mother. She is not sweet like Mary.
Her blue garments unloose small bats and owls.
How I would like to believe in tenderness –
The face of the effigy, gentled by candles,
Bending, on me in particular, its mild eyes.

[235]

I have fallen a long way. Clouds are flowering
Blue and mystical over the face of the stars.
Inside the church, the saints will be all blue,
Floating on their delicate feet over the cold pews,
Their hands and faces stiff with holiness.
The moon sees nothing of this. She is bald and wild.
And the message of the yew tree is blackness – blackness and
silence.

Mirror

I am silver and exact. I have no preconceptions.
Whatever I see I swallow immediately
Just as it is, unmisted by love or dislike.
I am not cruel, only truthful –
The eye of a little god, four-cornered.
Most of the time I meditate on the opposite wall.
It is pink, with speckles. I have looked at it so long
I think it is a part of my heart. But it flickers.
Faces and darkness separate us over and over.

Now I am a lake. A woman bends over me,
Searching my reaches for what she really is.
Then she turns to those liars, the candles or the moon.
I see her back, and reflect it faithfully.
She rewards me with tears and an agitation of hands.
I am important to her. She comes and goes.
Each morning it is her face that replaces the darkness.
In me she has drowned a young girl, and in me an old woman
Rises toward her day after day, like a terrible fish.

New Year on Dartmoor

This is newness: every little tawdry
Obstacle glass-wrapped and peculiar,
Glinting and clinking in a saint's falsetto. Only you
Don't know what to make of the sudden slippiness,
The blind, white, awful, inaccessible slant.
There's no getting up it by the words you know.
No getting up by elephant or wheel or shoe.
We have only come to look. You are too new
To want the world in a glass hat.

Among the Narcissi

Spry, wry, and grey as these March sticks,
Percy bows, in his blue peajacket, among the narcissi.
He is recuperating from something on the lung.

The narcissi, too, are bowing to some big thing:
It rattles their stars on the green hill where Percy
Nurses the hardship of his stitches, and walks and walks.

There is a dignity to this; there is a formality –
The flowers vivid as bandages, and the man mending.
They bow and stand: they suffer such attacks!

And the octogenarian loves the little flocks.
He is quite blue; the terrible wind tries his breathing.
The narcissi look up like children, quickly and whitely.

Poppies in July

Little poppies, little hell flames,
Do you do no harm?

You flicker. I cannot touch you.
I put my hands among the flames. Nothing burns.

And it exhausts me to watch you
Flickering like that, wrinkly and clear red, like the skin of a
mouth.

A mouth just bloodied.
Little bloody skirts!

There are fumes that I cannot touch.
Where are your opiates, your nauseous capsules?

If I could bleed, or sleep! –
If my mouth could marry a hurt like that!

Or your liquors seep to me, in this glass capsule,
Dulling and stilling.

But colourless. Colourless.

The Arrival of the Bee Box

I ordered this, this clean wood box
Square as a chair and almost too heavy to lift.
I would say it was the coffin of a midget
Or a square baby
Were there not such a din in it.

The box is locked, it is dangerous.
I have to live with it overnight
And I can't keep away from it.
There are no windows, so I can't see what is in there.
There is only a little grid, no exit.

I put my eye to the grid.
It is dark, dark,
With the swarmy feeling of African hands
Minute and shrunk for export,
Black and black, angrily clambering.

How can I let them out?
It is the noise that appals me most of all,
The unintelligible syllables.
It is like a Roman mob,
Small, taken one by one, but my god, together!

I lay my ear to furious Latin.
I am not a Caesar.
I have simply ordered a box of maniacs.
They can be sent back.
They can die, I need feed them nothing, I am the owner.

I wonder how hungry they are.
I wonder if they would forget me
If I just undid the locks and stood back and turned into a tree.
There is the laburnum, its blond colonnades,
And the petticoats of the cherry.

They might ignore me immediately
In my moon suit and funeral veil.
I am no source of honey
So why should they turn on me?
Tomorrow I will be sweet God, I will set them free.

The box is only temporary.

Fever 103°

Pure? What does it mean?
The tongues of hell
Are dull, dull as the triple

Tongues of dull, fat Cerberus
Who wheezes at the gate. Incapable
Of licking clean

The aguey tendon, the sin, the sin.
The tinder cries.
The indelible smell

Of a snuffed candle!
Love, love, the low smokes roll
From me like Isadora's scarves, I'm in a fright

One scarf will catch and anchor in the wheel.
Such yellow sullen smokes
Make their own element. They will not rise,

But trundle round the globe
Choking the aged and the meek,
The weak

Hothouse baby in its crib,
The ghastly orchid
Hanging its hanging garden in the air,

Devilish leopard!
Radiation turned it white
And killed it in an hour.

Greasing the bodies of adulterers
Like Hiroshima ash and eating in.
The sin. The sin.

Darling, all night
I have been flickering, off, on, off, on.
The sheets grow heavy as a lecher's kiss.

Three days. Three nights.
Lemon water, chicken
Water, water make me retch.

I am too pure for you or anyone.
Your body
Hurts me as the world hurts God. I am a lantern –

My head a moon
Of Japanese paper, my gold beaten skin
Infinitely delicate and infinitely expensive.

Does not my heat astound you. And my light.
All by myself I am a huge camellia
Glowing and coming and going, flush on flush.

I think I am going up,
I think I may rise –
The beads of hot metal fly, and I, love, I

Am a pure acetylene
Virgin
Attended by roses,

By kisses, by cherubim,
By whatever these pink things mean.
Not you, nor him

Not him, nor him
(My selves dissolving, old whore petticoats) –
To Paradise.

Poppies in October

Even the sun-clouds this morning cannot manage such skirts.
Nor the woman in the ambulance
Whose red heart blooms through her coat so astoundingly –

A gift, a love gift
Utterly unasked for
By a sky

Palely and flamily
Igniting its carbon monoxides, by eyes
Dulled to a halt under bowlers.

O my God, what am I
That these late mouths should cry open
In a forest of frost, in a dawn of cornflowers.

Lady Lazarus

I have done it again.
One year in every ten
I manage it –

A sort of walking miracle, my skin
Bright as a Nazi lampshade,
My right foot

A paperweight,
My face a featureless, fine
Jew linen.

Peel off the napkin
O my enemy.
Do I terrify? –

The nose, the eye pits, the full set of teeth?
The sour breath
Will vanish in a day.

Soon, soon the flesh
The grave cave ate will be
At home on me

And I a smiling woman.
I am only thirty.
And like the cat I have nine times to die.

This is Number Three.
What a trash
To annihilate each decade.

What a million filaments.
The peanut-crunching crowd
Shoves in to see

Them unwrap me hand and foot –
The big strip tease.
Gentlemen, ladies

These are my hands
My knees.
I may be skin and bone,

Nevertheless, I am the same, identical woman.
The first time it happened I was ten.
It was an accident.

The second time I meant
To last it out and not come back at all.
I rocked shut

As a seashell.
They had to call and call
And pick the worms off me like sticky pearls.

Dying
Is an art, like everything else.
I do it exceptionally well.

I do it so it feels like hell.
I do it so it feels real.
I guess you could say I've a call.

It's easy enough to do it in a cell.
It's easy enough to do it and stay put.
It's the theatrical

Comeback in broad day
To the same place, the same face, the same brute
Amused shout:

'A miracle!'
That knocks me out.
There is a charge

For the eyeing of my scars, there is a charge
For the hearing of my heart –
It really goes.

And there is a charge, a very large charge
For a word or a touch
Or a bit of blood

Or a piece of my hair or my clothes.
So, so, Herr Doktor.
So, Herr Enemy.

I am your opus,
I am your valuable,
The pure gold baby

That melts to a shriek.
I turn and burn.
Do not think I underestimate your great concern.

Ash, ash –
You poke and stir.
Flesh, bone, there is nothing there –

A cake of soap,
A wedding ring,
A gold filling.

Herr God, Herr Lucifer
Beware
Beware.

Out of the ash
I rise with my red hair
And I eat men like air.

Mary's Song

The Sunday lamb cracks in its fat.
The fat
Sacrifices its opacity . . .

A window, holy gold.
The fire makes it precious,
The same fire

Melting the tallow heretics,
Ousting the Jews.
Their thick palls float

Over the cicatrix of Poland, burnt-out
Germany.
They do not die.

Grey birds obsess my heart,
Mouth-ash, ash of eye.
They settle. On the high

Precipice
That emptied one man into space
The ovens glowed like heavens, incandescent.

It is a heart,
This holocaust I walk in,
O golden child the world will kill and eat.

Sheep in Fog

The hills step off into whiteness.
People or stars
Regard me sadly, I disappoint them.

The train leaves a line of breath.
O slow
Horse the colour of rust,

Hooves, dolorous bells –
All morning the
Morning has been blackening,

A flower left out.
My bones hold a stillness, the far
Fields melt my heart.

They threaten
To let me through to a heaven
Starless and fatherless, a dark water.

Paralytic

It happens. Will it go on? –
My mind a rock,
No fingers to grip, no tongue,
My god the iron lung

That loves me, pumps
My two
Dust bags in and out,
Will not

Let me relapse
While the day outside glides by like ticker tape.
The night brings violets,
Tapestries of eyes,

Lights,
The soft anonymous
Talkers: 'You all right?'
The starched, inaccessible breast.

Dead egg, I lie
Whole
On a whole world I cannot touch,
At the white, tight

Drum of my sleeping couch
Photographs visit me –
My wife, dead and flat, in 1920 furs,
Mouth full of pearls,

Two girls
As flat as she, who whisper 'We're your daughters.'
The still waters
Wrap my lips,

Eyes, nose and ears,
A clear
Cellophane I cannot crack.
On my bare back

I smile, a buddha, all
Wants, desire
Falling from me like rings
Hugging their lights.

The claw
Of the magnolia,
Drunk on its own scents,
Asks nothing of life.

Kindness

Kindness glides about my house.
Dame Kindness, she is so nice!
The blue and red jewels of her rings smoke
In the windows, the mirrors
Are filling with smiles.

What is so real as the cry of a child?
A rabbit's cry may be wilder
But it has no soul.
Sugar can cure everything, so Kindness says.
Sugar is a necessary fluid,

Its crystals a little poultice.
O kindness, kindness
Sweetly picking up pieces!
My Japanese silks, desperate butterflies,
May be pinned any minute, anaesthetized.

And here you come, with a cup of tea
Wreathed in steam.
The blood jet is poetry,
There is no stopping it.
You hand me two children, two roses.

Balloons

Since Christmas they have lived with us,
Guileless and clear,
Oval soul-animals,
Taking up half the space,
Moving and rubbing on the silk

Invisible air drifts,
Giving a shriek and pop
When attacked, then scooting to rest, barely trembling.
Yellow cathead, blue fish –
Such queer moons we live with

Instead of dead furniture!
Straw mats, white walls
And these travelling
Globes of thin air, red, green,
Delighting

The heart like wishes or free
Peacocks blessing
Old ground with a feather
Beaten in starry metals.
Your small

Brother is making
His balloon squeak like a cat.
Seeming to see
A funny pink world he might eat on the other side of it,
He bites,

Then sits
Back, fat jug
Contemplating a world clear as water,
A red
Shred in his little fist.

Edge

The woman is perfected.
Her dead

Body wears the smile of accomplishment,
The illusion of a Greek necessity

Flows in the scrolls of her toga,
Her bare

Feet seem to be saying:
We have come so far, it is over.

Each dead child coiled, a white serpent,
One at each little

Pitcher of milk, now empty.
She has folded

Them back into her body as petals
Of a rose close when the garden

Stiffens and odours bleed
From the sweet, deep throats of the night flower.

The moon has nothing to be sad about,
Staring from her hood of bone.

She is used to this sort of thing.
Her blacks crackle and drag.

ANNE STEVENSON

By the Boat House, Oxford

They belong here in their own quenched country.
I had forgotten nice women could be so nice,
smiling beside large sons on the makeshift quay,
frail, behind pale faces and hurt eyes.

Their husbands are plainly superior, with them, without them.
Their boys wear privilege like a clear inheritance, easily.
(Now a swan's neck couples with its own reflection,
making in the simple water a perfect 3.)

The punts seem resigned to an unexciting mooring.
But the women? It's hard to tell. Do their fine grey hairs
and filament lips approve or disdain the loving
that living alone, or else lonely in pairs, impairs?

Himalayan Balsam

Orchid-lipped, loose-jointed, purplish, indolent flowers,
with a ripe smell of peaches, like a girl's breath through lipstick,
delicate and coarse in the weedlap of late summer rivers,
dishevelled, weak-stemmed, common as brambles, as love which

subtracts us from seasons, their courtships and murders,
(*Meta segmentata* in her web, and the male waiting,
between blossom and violent blossom, meticulous spiders
repeated in gossamer, and the slim males waiting . . .)

Fragrance too rich for keeping, too light to remember,
like grief for the cat's sparrow and the wild gull's
beach-hatched embryo. (She ran from the reaching water
with the broken egg in her hand, but the clamped bill

refused brandy and grubs, a shred too naked and perilous for
life offered freely in cardboard boxes, little windowsill
coffins for bird death, kitten death, squirrel death, summer
repeated and ended in heartbreak, in the sad small funerals.)

Sometimes, shaping bread or scraping potatoes for supper,
I have stood in the kitchen, transfixed by what I'd call love
if love were a whiff, a wanting for no particular lover,
no child, or baby or creature. 'Love, dear love'

I could cry to these scent-spilling ragged flowers
and mean nothing but 'no', by that word's breadth,
to their evident going, their important descent through red
                                                    towering
stalks to the riverbed. It's not, as I thought, that death

creates love. More that love knows death. Therefore
tears, therefore poems, therefore the long stone sobs of
                                                    cathedrals
that speak to no ferret or fox, that prevent no massacre.
(I am combing abundant leaves from these icy shallows.)

Love, it was you who said, 'Murder the killer
we have to call life and we'd be a bare planet under a dead sun.'
Then I loved you with the usual soft lust of October
that says 'yes' to the coming winter and a summoning odour of
                                                    balsam.

Suicide

There was no hole in the universe to fit him.
He felt it as he fooled around. No rim,
no closet, nowhere to hide. The moon
also was fooling. He told
the girl and she giggled. 'As much for you
as for anyone.' But it wasn't true.

Spiders with their eight eyes, snails had more to do.

'When I said I wouldn't kiss him
he said he'd slash his wrists.
He was always saying stupid things like this.'

He saw himself entering women.
Wide open hay-scented barn, transistor on,
heavy rhythm of drums to draw him in.
And then that smallness, tiny loop at the end
where a slipknot tightened over light until a fist
struck. Darkness swelled around him like a breast.

The noose around his neck had been some help –
a childish mouth, a joke, an easy jump.
He was free as air when the girl's father found him,
returning from an evening out with friends.

Giving Rabbit to my Cat Bonnie

Pretty Bonnie, you are quick as a rabbit,
though your tail's longer,
emphasizing suppressed disapproval,
and your ears are shorter – two
radar detectors set on swivels
either side of your skull, and your yawn
is a view of distant white spires – not
the graveyard jaw of this poor dead naked pink

rabbit, who like you, was a
technological success, inheriting a snazzy
fur coat, pepper-and-salt coloured, cosy,
and beautiful fur shoes with spiked toes.
You're both of you
better dressed than I am for most occasions.
Take off your shoes and suits, though,
what have you got?

Look puss, I've brought us a rabbit for supper.
I bought it in a shop.
The butcher was haggis-shaped, ham-coloured,
not a bit like you. His ears
were two fungi on the slab of his head.
He had a fat, flat face.
But he took your brother rabbit off a hook
and spread him on the counter like a rug,

and slice, slice, scarcely looking,
pulled the lovely skin off like a bag.
So, Bonnie, all I've brought us is food
in this silly pink shape – more like me, really.
I'll make a wine sauce with mushrooms, but will
you want this precious broken heart? this perfect liver?
See, protected in these back pockets, jewels?
Bonnie. What are you eating? Dear Bonnie, consider!

[255]

FLEUR ADCOCK

The Ex-queen among the Astronomers

They serve revolving saucer eyes,
dishes of stars; they wait upon
huge lenses hung aloft to frame
the slow procession of the skies.

They calculate, adjust, record,
watch transits, measure distances.
They carry pocket telescopes
to spy through when they walk abroad.

Spectra possess their eyes; they face
upwards, alert for meteorites,
cherishing little glassy worlds:
receptacles for outer space.

But she, exile, expelled, ex-queen,
swishes among the men of science
waiting for cloudy skies, for nights
when constellations can't be seen.

She wears the rings he let her keep;
she walks as she was taught to walk
for his approval, years ago.
His bitter features taunt her sleep.

And so when these have laid aside
their telescopes, when lids are closed
between machine and sky, she seeks
terrestrial bodies to bestride.

She plucks this one or that among
the astronomers, and is become
his canopy, his occultation;
she sucks at earlobe, penis, tongue

mouthing the tubes of flesh; her hair
crackles, her eyes are comet-sparks.
She brings the distant briefly close
above his dreamy abstract stare.

Blue Glass

The underworld of children becomes the overworld
when Janey or Sharon shuts the attic door
on a sunny afternoon and tiptoes in sandals
that softly waffle-print the dusty floor

to the cluttered bed below the skylight,
managing not to sneeze as she lifts
newspapers, boxes, gap-stringed tennis-racquets
and a hamster's cage to the floor, and shifts

the tasselled cover to make a clean surface
and a pillow to be tidy under her head
before she straightens, mouths the dark sentence,
and lays herself out like a mummy on the bed.

Her wrists are crossed. The pads of her fingertips
trace the cold glass emblem where it lies
like a chain of hailstones melting in the dips
above her collarbones. She needs no eyes

to see it: the blue bead necklace, of sapphire
or lapis, or of other words she knows
which might mean blueness: amethyst, azure,
chalcedony can hardly say how it glows.

She stole it. She tells herself that she found it.
It's hers now. It owns her. She slithers among
its globular teeth, skidding on blue pellets.
Ice-beads flare and blossom on her tongue,

turn into flowers, populate the spaces
around and below her. The attic has become
her bluebell wood. Among their sappy grasses
the light-fringed gas-flames of bluebells hum.

They lift her body like a cloud of petals.
High now, floating, this is what she sees:
granular bark six inches from her eyeballs;
the wood of rafters is the wood of trees.

Her breathing moistens the branches' undersides;
the sunlight in an interrupted shaft
warms her legs and lulls her as she rides
on air, a slender and impossible raft

of bones and flesh; and whether it is knowledge
or a limpid innocence on which she feeds
for power hasn't mattered. She turns the necklace
kindly in her fingers, and soothes the beads.

JEAN VALENTINE

A Bride's Hours

for Arthur Platt

1 DAWN

I try to hold your face in my mind's million eyes
But nothing hangs together. My spirit lies
Around my will like an extra skin
I cannot fill or shake.
My eyes in Bachrach's rectangle look in.
I, who was once at the core of the world,
Whose childish outline held like a written word,
Am frozen in blur: my body, waiting, pours
Over its centaur dreams, and drowns, and wakes
To terror of man and horse.

2 THE BATH

My sisters walk around touching things, or loll
On the bed with last month's *New Yorkers*. My skin,
Beaded with bath-oil, gleams like a hot-house fake:
My body holds me like an empty bowl.
It is three, it is four, it is time to come in
From thinking about the cake to eat the cake.
My sisters' voices whir like cardboard birds
On sticks: married, they flutter and wheel to find
In this misted looking-glass their own lost words,
In the exhaled smoke.
                              There isn't a sound,
Even the shadows compose like waiting wings.
I am the hollow circle closed by the ring.

3 NIGHT

I am thrown open like a child's damp hand
In sleep. You turn your back in sleep, unmanned.
How can I be so light, at the core of things?
My way was long and crooked to your hand!
What could your jewelled glove command
But flight of my stone wings?
Our honeymoon lake, ignoring the lit-up land,
Shows blank Orion where to dip his hand.

Sex

All the years waiting, the whole, barren, young
Life long. The gummy yearning
All night long for the far white oval
Moving on the ceiling;
The hand on the head, the hand in hand;
The gummy pages of dirty books by flashlight,
Blank as those damaged classical groins;

Diffusion of leaves on the night sky,
The queer, sublunar walks.
And the words: the lily, the flame, the truelove knot,
Forget-me-not; coming, going,
Having, taking, lying with,
Knowing, dying;
The old king's polar sword,
The wine glass shattered on the stone floor.

And the thing itself not the thing itself,
But a metaphor.

Orpheus and Eurydice

'What we spent, we had.
What we had, we have.
What we lost, we leave.'

—Epitaph for his wife and himself,
by the Duke of Devon, 12th century

I

You. You running across the field.

A hissing second, not a word,
and there it was, our underworld:
behind your face another, and another,
and I

away.

– And you alive: staring,
almost smiling;

hearing them come down, tearing
air from air.

II

'This dark is everywhere'
we said, and called it light,
coming to ourselves.
                    Fear
has at me, dearest. Even this night
drags down. The moon's gone. Someone
shakes an old black camera-cloth
in front of our eyes.
Yours glint like a snowman's eyes.
We just look on, at each other.

[261]

What we had, we have. They circle down.
You draw them down like flies.
You laugh, we run
over a red field, turning at the end to blue air, –
you turning, turning again! the river
tossing a shoe up, a handful of hair.

JUNE JORDAN

The Reception

Doretha wore the short blue lace last night
and William watched her drinking so she fight
with him in flying collar slim-jim orange
tie and alligator belt below the navel pants uptight

'I flirt. You hear me? Yes I flirt.
Been on my pretty knees all week
to clean the rich white downtown dirt
the greedy garbage money reek.

I flirt. Damned right. You look at me.'
But William watched her carefully
his mustache shaky she could see
him jealous, 'which is how he always be

at parties.' Clementine and Wilhelmina
looked at trouble in the light blue lace
and held to George while Roosevelt Senior
circled by the yella high and bitterly light blue face

he liked because she worked
the crowded room like clay like molding men
from dust to muscle jerked
and arms and shoulders moving when

she moved. The Lord Almighty Seagrams bless
Doretha in her short blue dress
and Roosevelt waiting for his chance:
a true gut-funky blues to make her really dance.

[263]

Clock on Hancock Street

In the wintertime my father wears a hat
a green straw laundry shrunken hat
to open up the wartime iron gate
requiring a special key he keeps
in case he hears the seldom basement bell
a long key cost him seven dollars
took three days to make

around the corner

in the house no furniture remains
he gave away the piano
and the hard-back parlor couch the rosy rug
and the double bed
the large black bureau
china cups and saucers
from Japan

His suitcase is a wooden floor
where magazines called *Life*
smell like a garbage truck
that travels farther than he
reasonably can expect
to go

His face seems small or
loose and bearded in the afternoon

Today he was complaining about criminals:

They will come and steal the heavy red umbrella stand

from upstairs in the hallway
where my mother used to walk

and talk to him

[264]

JUDITH RODRIGUEZ

The Handloom

Square as a seed-box, in their attic stands
the frame of clear-lacquered wood with its woollen crop
the colours of growing, runners and pods and tendrils
winding back to a stop
in the flat slotted seeds shaped to a busy hand:

hers, that threaded shuttles into the making
of this bulked stitchery, then lost its skill and self-
possession. In a shaking of heads, quite straight and slack
death ranged her; unravelled flesh
and bone part well-disposed. Puzzles of leave-taking

tangle these pious others; they cringe from her foiled
scrollings and bulbings, that fold in no formal promise.
They never will finish the work of the suicide,
though meaning to sometime, and honest:
the fitter and turner, his wife who sings, and their child.

How Come the Truck-loads?

Somehow the tutorial takes an unplanned direction:
anti-Semitism.
A scholastic devil advances the suggestion
that two sides can be found to every question:

[265]

Right.
Now, who's an anti-Semite?
One hand.
Late thirties, in the 1960s. Bland.
Let's see now; tell us, on what texts or Jews
do you base your views?
There was a landlord, from Poland, that I had.
Bad?
A shrug. Well, what did he do?
Pretty mean chasing up rent. Ah. Tough.
And who
else? No one else. One's enough.

Eskimo Occasion

I am in my Eskimo-hunting-song mood,
Aha!
The lawn is tundra   the car will not start
the sunlight is an avalanche   we are avalanche-struck at our
                                                                breakfast
struck with sunlight through glass   me and my spoon-fed
                                                                daughters
out of this world in our kitchen.

I will sing the song of my daughter-hunting,
Oho!
The waves lay down   the ice grew strong
I sang the song   of dark water under ice
the song of winter fishing   the magic for seal rising
among the ancestor-masks.

I waited by water to dream new spirits,
Hoo!
The water spoke   the ice shouted
the sea opened   the sun made young shadows
they breathed my breathing   I took them from deep water
I brought them fur-warmed home.

I am dancing the years of the two great hunts,
Ya-hay!
It was I who waited   cold in the wind-break
I stamp like the bear   I call like the wind of the thaw
I leap like the sea spring-running.   My sunstruck daughters
                                                splutter
and chuckle and bang their spoons:

Mummy is singing at breakfast and dancing!
So big!

GILLIAN CLARKE

Baby-sitting

I am sitting in a strange room listening
For the wrong baby. I don't love
This baby. She is sleeping a snuffly
Roseate, bubbling sleep; she is fair;
She is a perfectly acceptable child.
I am afraid of her. If she wakes
She will hate me. She will shout
Her hot, midnight rage, her nose
Will stream disgustingly and the perfume
Of her breath will fail to enchant me.

To her I will represent absolute
Abandonment. For her it will be worse
Than for the lover cold in lonely
Sheets; worse than for the woman who waits
A moment to collect her dignity
Beside the bleached bone in the terminal ward.
As she rises sobbing from the monstrous land
Stretching for milk-familiar comforting,
She will find me and between us two
It will not come. It will not come.

MARGARET ATWOOD

Game after Supper

This is before electricity,
it is when there were porches.

On the sagging porch an old man
is rocking. The porch is wooden,

the house is wooden and grey;
in the living room which smells of
smoke and mildew, soon
the woman will light the kerosene lamp.

There is a barn but I am not in the barn;
there is an orchard too, gone bad,
its apples like soft cork
but I am not there either.

I am hiding in the long grass
with my two dead cousins,
the membrane grown already
across their throats.

We hear crickets and our own hearts
close to our ears;
though we giggle, we are afraid.

From the shadows around
the corner of the house
a tall man is coming to find us:

He will be an uncle,
if we are lucky.

Habitation

Marriage is not
a house or even a tent

it is before that, and colder:

the edge of the forest, the edge
of the desert
              the unpainted stairs
at the back where we squat
outside, eating popcorn

the edge of the receding glacier

where painfully and with wonder
at having survived even
this far

we are learning to make fire

Woman Skating

A lake sunken among
cedar and black spruce hills;
late afternoon.

On the ice a woman skating,
jacket sudden
red against the white,

concentrating on moving
in perfect circles.

(actually she is my mother, she is
over at the outdoor skating rink
near the cemetery. On three sides
of her there are streets of brown
brick houses; cars go by; on the
fourth side is the park building.
The snow banked around the rink
is grey with soot. She never skates
here. She's wearing a sweater and
faded maroon earmuffs, she has
taken off her gloves)

Now near the horizon
the enlarged pink sun swings down.
Soon it will be zero.

With arms wide the skater
turns, leaving her breath like a diver's
trail of bubbles.

Seeing the ice
as what it is, water:
seeing the months
as they are, the years
in sequence occurring
underfoot, watching
the miniature human
figure balanced on steel
needles (those compasses
floated in saucers) on time
sustained, above
time circling: miracle

Over all I place
a glass bell

Siren Song

This is the one song everyone
would like to learn: the song
that is irresistible:

the song that forces men
to leap overboard in squadrons
even though they see the beached skulls

the song nobody knows
because anyone who has heard it
is dead, and the others can't remember.

Shall I tell you the secret
and if I do, will you get me
out of this bird suit?

I don't enjoy it here
squatting on this island
looking picturesque and mythical

with these two feathery maniacs,
I don't enjoy singing
this trio, fatal and valuable.

I will tell the secret to you,
to you, only to you.
Come closer. This song

is a cry for help: Help me!
Only you, only you can,
you are unique

at last. Alas
it is a boring song
but it works every time.

GWENDOLYN MacEWEN

Sea Things

I've been giving a lot of thought
to shellfish and sponges and those
half-plant half-animal things that go
flump flump on the sea floor, also
a funny thing shaped like a pyramid
which spends all its life
buried in the sand upside-down
and has no friends.

And because I know nothing
about the sea I worry
about how they're finding their food
or making love, or for that matter
if they have anything to make love with.

I open a can of oysters
and see them all lying there, lying there
naked and embryonic, and wonder
how long I can go on worrying about things
that creep around miles below my eye
beneath tons of black water

With their hopes and fears and hungers
and their attempts to better themselves
and the secret brains or pearls they keep
protected in their shells.

I've been giving them a lot of thought
but I do not really want to know them,
for they flung me forth, a nuisance in their midst
with my mind and complex hungers
crashing on the high white beaches of the world.

You Cannot Do This

you cannot do this to them, these are my people;
I am not speaking of poetry, I am not speaking of art.
you cannot do this to them, these are my people.
you cannot hack away the horizon in front of their eyes.

the tomb, articulate, will record your doing;
I will record it also, this is not art.
this is a kind of science, a kind of hobby,
a kind of personal vice like coin collecting.

it has something to do with horses
and signet rings and school trophies;
it has something to do with the pride of the loins;
it has something to do with good food and music,
and something to do with power, and dancing.
you cannot do this to them, these are my people.

The Virgin Warrior

When we rested between marches, I read Aristophanes
In the original Greek. I also had
                              Morte d'Arthur, and
The Oxford Book of English Verse.
                              Then came the day
            of the camel charge; we surged forward, swords
            raised like exclamation marks, and
            purple banners flying.
When the enemy became real, I got terribly excited
            and shot my camel through the head
            by accident, flew to the ground
And lay there with her as the army leapt over us,

Thinking, in lines as long as a camel's stride, of Kipling.

EILÉAN NI CHUILLEANÁIN

Swineherd

'When all this is over,' said the swineherd,
'I mean to retire, where
Nobody will have heard about my special skills
And conversation is mainly about the weather.

I intend to learn how to make coffee, at least as well
As the Portuguese lay-sister in the kitchen
And polish the brass fenders every day.
I want to lie awake at night
Listening to cream crawling to the top of the jug
And the water lying soft in the cistern.

I want to see an orchard where the trees grow in straight lines
And the yellow fox finds shelter between the navy-blue trunks,
Where it gets dark early in summer
And the apple-blossom is allowed to wither on the bough.'

Letter to Pearse Hutchinson

I saw the islands in a ring all round me
And the twilight sea travelling past
Uneasy still. Lightning over Mount Gabriel:
At such a distance no sound of thunder.
The mackerel just taken
Battered the floor, and at my elbow
The waves disputed with the engine.
Equally grey, the headlands
Crept round the rim of the sea.

Going anywhere fast is a trap:
This water music ransacked my mind
And started it growing again in a new perspective
And like the sea that burrows and soaks
In the swamps and crevices beneath
Made a circle out of good and ill.

So I accepted all the sufferings of the poor,
The old maid and the old whore
And the bull trying to remember
What it was made him courageous
As life goes to ground in one of its caves,
And I accepted the way love
Poured down a cul-de-sac
Is never seen again.

There was plenty of time while the sea-water
Nosed across the ruinous ocean floor
Inquiring for the ruinous door of the womb
And found the soul of Vercingetorix
Cramped in a jam jar
Who was starved to death in a dry cistern
In Rome, in 46 BC.

Do not expect to feel so free on land.

TESS GALLAGHER

Instructions to the Double

So now it's your turn,
little mother of silences, little
father of half-belief. Take up
this face, these daily rounds
with a cabbage under each arm
convincing the multitudes
that a well-made-anything
could save them. Take up
most of all, these hands
trained to an ornate piano
in a house on the other side
of the country.

I'm staying here
without music, without
applause. I'm not going
to wait up for you. Take
your time. Take mine
too. Get into some trouble
I'll have to account for. Walk
into some bars alone
with a slit in your skirt. Let
the men follow you on the street
with their clumsy propositions, their
loud hatreds of this and that. Keep
walking. Keep your head
up. They are calling to you – slut, mother,
virgin, whore, daughter, adulteress, lover,
mistress, bitch, wife, cunt, harlot,

betrothed, Jezebel, Messalina, Diana,
Bathsheba, Rebecca, Lucretia, Mary,
Magdelena, Ruth, you – Niobe,
woman of the tombs.

Don't stop for anything, not
a caress or a promise. Go
to the temple of the poets, not
the one like a run-down country club,
but the one on fire
with so much it wants
to be done with. Say all the last words
and the first: hello, goodbye, yes,
I, no, please, always, never.

If anyone from the country club
asks if you write poems, say
your name is Lizzie Borden.
Show him your axe, the one
they gave you with a silver
blade, your name engraved there
like a whisper of their own.

If anyone calls you a witch,
burn for him; if anyone calls you
less or more than you are
let him burn for you.

It's a dangerous mission. You
could die out there. You
could live for ever.

Black Silk

She was cleaning – there is always
that to do – when she found,
at the top of the closet, his old
silk vest. She called me
to look at it, unrolling it carefully
like something live
might fall out. Then we spread it
on the kitchen table and smoothed
the wrinkles down, making our hands
heavy until its shape against formica
came back and the little tips
that would have pointed to his pockets
lay flat. The buttons were all there.
I held my arms out and she
looped the wide armholes over
them. 'That's one thing I never
wanted to be,' she said, 'a man.'
I went into the bathroom to see
how I looked in the sheen and
sadness. Wind chimes
off-key in the alcove. Then her
crying so I stood back in the sink-light
where the porcelain had been staring. Time
to go to her, I thought, with that
other mind, and stood still.

Each Bird Walking

Not while, but long after he had told me,
I thought of him, washing his mother, his
bending over the bed and taking back
the covers. There was a basin of water
and he dipped a washrag in and
out of the basin, the rag
dripping a little onto the sheet as he
turned from the bedside to the nightstand
and back, there being no place

on her body he shouldn't touch because
he had to and she helped him, moving
the little she could, lifting so he could
wipe under her arms, a dipping motion
in the hollow. Then working up from
the feet, around the ankles, over the
knees. And this last, opening
her thighs and running the rag firmly
and with the cleaning thought
up through her crotch, between the lips,
over the V of thin hairs –

as though he were a mother
who had the excuse of cleaning to touch
with love and indifference
the secret parts of her child, to graze
the sleepy sexlessness in its waiting
to find out what to do for the sake
of the body, for the sake of what only
the body can do for itself.

So his hand, softly at the place
of his birth-light. And she, eyes deepened
and closed in the dim room.
And because he told me her death as
important to his being with her,
I could love him another way. Not
of the body alone, or of its making,
but carried in the white spires of trembling
until what spirit, what breath we were
was shaken from us. Small then,
the word *holy*.

He turned her on her stomach
and washed the blades of her shoulders, the
small of her back. 'That's good,' she said,
'that's enough.'

On our lips that morning, the tart juice
of the mothers, so strong in remembrance, no
asking, no giving, and what you said, this
being the end of our loving, so as not to hurt
the closer one to you, made me look
to see what was left of us
with our sex taken away. 'Tell me,' I said,
'something I can't forget.' Then the story of
your mother, and when you finished
I said, 'That's good, that's enough.'

LOUISE GLÜCK

For Jane Myers

Sap rises from the sodden ditch
and glues two green ears to the dead
birch twig. Perilous beauty –
and already Jane is digging out
her colored tennis shoes,
one mauve, one yellow, like large crocuses.

And by the laundromat
the Bartletts in their tidy yard –

as though it were not
wearying, wearying

to hear in the bushes
the mild harping of the breeze,
the daffodils flocking and honking –

Look how the bluet falls apart, mud
pockets the seed.
Months, years, then the dull blade of the wind.
It is spring! We are going to die!

And now April raises up her plaque of flowers
and the heart
expands to admit its adversary.

Gratitude

Do not think I am not grateful for your small
kindness to me.
I like small kindnesses.
In fact I actually prefer them to the more
substantial kindness that is always eyeing you,
like a large animal on a rug,
until your whole life reduces
to nothing but waking up morning after morning
cramped, and the bright sun shining on its tusks.

The Undertaking

The darkness lifts, imagine, in your lifetime.
There you are – cased in clean bark you drift
through weaving rushes, fields flooded with cotton.
You are free. The river films with lilies,
shrubs appear, shoots thicken into palm. And now
all fear gives way: the light
looks after you, you feel the waves' goodwill
as arms widen over the water; Love,

the key is turned. Extend yourself –
it is the Nile, the sun is shining,
everywhere you turn is luck.

Descending Figure

1 THE WANDERER

At twilight I went into the street.
The sun hung low in the iron sky,
ringed with cold plumage.
If I could write to you
about this emptiness –
Along the curb, groups of children
were playing in the dry leaves.
Long ago, at this hour, my mother stood
at the lawn's edge, holding my little sister.
Everyone was gone; I was playing
in the dark street with my other sister,
whom death had made so lonely.
Night after night we watched the screened porch
filling with a gold, magnetic light.
Why was she never called?
Often I would let my own name glide past me
though I craved its protection.

2 THE SICK CHILD
Rijksmuseum

A small child
is ill, has wakened.
It is winter, past midnight
in Antwerp. Above a wooden chest,
the stars shine.
And the child
relaxes in her mother's arms.
The mother does not sleep;
she stares

[284]

fixedly into the bright museum.
By spring the child will die.
Then it is wrong, wrong
to hold her –
Let her be alone,
without memory, as the others wake
terrified, scraping the dark
paint from their faces.

3 FOR MY SISTER

Far away my sister is moving in her crib.
The dead ones are like that,
always the last to quiet.

Because, however long they lie in the earth,
they will not learn to speak
but remain uncertainly pressing against the wooden bars,
so small the leaves hold them down.

Now, if she had a voice,
the cries of hunger would be beginning.
I should go to her;
perhaps if I sang very softly,
her skin so white,
her head covered with black feathers . . .

Dedication to Hunger

1 FROM THE SUBURBS

They cross the yard
and at the back door
the mother sees with pleasure
how alike they are, father and daughter –
I know something of that time.
The little girl purposefully
swinging her arms, laughing
her stark laugh:

It should be kept secret, that sound.
It means she's realized
that he never touches her.
She is a child; he could touch her
if he wanted to.

2 GRANDMOTHER

'Often I would stand at the window –
your grandfather
was a young man then –
waiting, in the early evening.'

That is what marriage is.
I watch the tiny figure
changing to a man
as he moves toward her,
the last light rings in his hair.
I do not question
their happiness. And he rushes in
with his young man's hunger,
so proud to have taught her that:
his kiss would have been
clearly tender –

Of course, of course. Except
it might as well have been
his hand over her mouth.

3   EROS

To be male, always
to go to women
and be taken back
into the pierced flesh:

       I suppose
memory is stirred.
And the girl child
who wills herself
into her father's arms
likewise loved him
second. Nor is she told
what need to express.
There is a look one sees,
the mouth somehow desperate –

Because the bond
cannot be proven.

4   THE DEVIATION

It begins quietly
in certain female children:
the fear of death, taking as its form
dedication to hunger,
because a woman's body
is a grave; it will accept
anything. I remember
lying in bed at night
touching the soft, digressive breasts,
touching, at fifteen,

[287]

the interfering flesh
that I would sacrifice
until the limbs were free
of blossom and subterfuge: I felt
what I feel now, aligning these words –
it is the same need to perfect,
of which death is the mere by-product.

5 SACRED OBJECTS

Today in the field I saw
the hard, active buds of the dogwood
and wanted, as we say, to capture them,
to make them eternal. That is the premise
of renunciation: the child,
having no self to speak of,
comes to life in denial –

I stood apart in that achievement,
in that power to expose
the underlying body, like a god
for whose deed
there is no parallel in the natural world.

The Gift

Lord, You may not recognize me
speaking for someone else.
I have a son. He is
so little, so ignorant.
He likes to stand
at the screen door, calling
oggie, oggie, entering
language, and sometimes
a dog will stop and come up
the walk, perhaps
accidentally. May he believe
this is not an accident?
At the screen
welcoming each beast
in love's name, Your emissary.

SANDRA McPHERSON

1943

I was born the year of the gray pennies.
They'll find me in another layer, the skull
above the deviating Lincoln heads

worth ten or fifteen cents by now.
The smile won't be in the bone,
so they will think that I've depreciated.

But that money didn't last. Gray did
and camouflaged our war,
woodchucks, catbirds –

the year of our birth sank beneath us.
The bank was rock.
On top of me are falling all the saved.

Children

She will run to you for love whoever
you are, you who'd forgotten what you look like.
She keeps a book of forms in her arms,
like a fitter exact on waists.

And perhaps I'll have to pull her from
celebrating her birth between your legs
although she is my only child
and good at it and best of all the children

you don't have. You know her face
can't be yours. But let me become a stranger,
not act myself, beat on the mirror and cry –
she sees I look like her alone.

And sticking her face in mine, smearing my
lipstick with her index finger, igniting
the pale mustache, drawing the seeing mirror
of her glasses down oil

on my cheeks, she hangs my picture
for ever in her head. So that she always
sees to me when I am down
and thinks the way to raise me is

to climb aboard me toe for toe, palm
lidding palm so I can't withdraw
or go out of our single mind
to have another child.

ELLEN BRYANT VOIGT

Why She Says No

Two friends at the close of summer.
On the path, the birds quicken.
While he talks,
he strokes her arm in one direction
as if it had a nap of feathers.
How handsomely the heart's valves
lie open for the bloodrush.
How her body also begins to open.
At the edge of the woods, they pass
goldenrod and lupin, the tall thin weeds
supple as a whale's teeth
conducting the avid fish to the interior.

She is not the mouth, whatever you think
and even though she craves
this closeness, its rich transfusion.
Desire is the mouth, the manipulating heart,
the wing. Above her,
the branches of the pines, their quilled expanse
blanketing the subtler vegetation.

CAROL RUMENS

An Easter Garland

I

The flowers did not seem to unfurl from slow bulbs.
They were suddenly there,
shivering swimmers on the edge of a gala
– nude whites and yellows shocking the raw air.
They'd switched themselves on like streetlamps
waking at dawn, feeling wrong,
to blaze nervously all day at the chalky sky.
Are they masks, the frills on bruised babies?
I can't believe in them,
as I can't believe in the spruces and lawns and bricks
they publicize, the misted light of front lounges
twinned all the way down the road,
twinned like their occupants, little weather-house people
who hide inside and do not show their tears
– the moisture that drives one sadly to a doorway.

II

My father explained the workings of the weather-house
as if he seriously loved such things,
told me why Grandpa kept a blackening tress
of seaweed in the hall.
He was an expert on atmosphere,
having known a weight of dampness
– the fog in a sick brother's lungs
where he lost his childhood; later, the soft squalls
of marriage and the wordier silences.

In the atmosphere of the fire
that took him back to bone
and beyond bone, he smiled.
The cellophaned flowers outside
went a slower way, their sweat
dappling the linings of their glassy hoods.

III

My orphaned grass
is standing on tiptoe to look for you.
Your last gift to a work-shy daughter
was to play out and regather
the slow thread of your breath
behind the rattling blades,
crossing always to darker green,
till the lawn was a well-washed quilt
drying, the palest on the line,
and you rested over the handlebars
like a schoolboy, freewheeling
through your decades of green-scented, blue,
suburban English twilights.

IV

In the lonely garden of the page,
something has happened to your silence.
The stone cloud has rolled off.
You make yourself known,
as innocently abrupt
as the flared wings of the almond,
cherry, magnolia;
and I, though stupid with regret,
would not be far wrong
if I took you for the gardener.

CAROL RUMENS

Geography Lesson

Here we have the sea of children; here
A tiny piece of Europe with dark hair.
She's crying. I am sitting next to her.

Thirty yellow suns blobbed on cheap paper,
Thirty skies blue as a Smith's salt-wrapper
Are fading in the darkness of this weeper.

She's Czechoslovakia. And all the desks
Are shaking now. The classroom window cracks
And melts. I've caught her sobs like chicken-pox.

Czechoslovakia, though I've never seen
Your cities, I have somehow touched your skin.
You're all the hurt geography I own.

EAVAN BOLAND

The Famine Road

'Idle as trout in light Colonel Jones,
these Irish, give them no coins at all; their bones
need toil, their characters no less.' Trevelyan's
seal blooded the deal table. The Relief
Committee deliberated: 'Might it be safe,
Colonel, to give them roads, roads to force
from nowhere, going nowhere of course?'

> *'one out of every ten and then*
> *another third of those again*
> *women – in a case like yours.'*

Sick, directionless they worked; fork, stick
were iron years away; after all could
they not blood their knuckles on rock, suck
April hailstones for water and for food?
Why for that, cunning as housewives, each eyed –
as if at a corner butcher – the other's buttock.

> *'anything may have caused it, spores,*
> *a childhood accident; one sees*
> *day after day these mysteries.'*

Dusk: they will work tomorrow without him.
They know it and walk clear; he has become
a typhoid pariah, his blood tainted, although
he shares it with some there. No more than snow
attends its own flakes where they settle
and melt, will they pray by his death rattle.

'You never will, never you know
but take it well woman, grow
your garden, keep house, good-bye.'

'It has gone better than we expected, Lord
Trevelyan, sedition, idleness, cured
in one; from parish to parish, field to field,
the wretches work till they are quite worn,
then fester by their work; we march the corn
to the ships in peace; this Tuesday I saw bones
out of my carriage window, your servant Jones.'

'Barren, never to know the load
of his child in you, what is your body
now if not a famine road?'

WENDY COPE

Depression

You lie, snail-like, on your stomach –
I dare not speak or touch,
Knowing too well the ways of our kind –
The retreat, the narrowing spiral.

We are both convinced it is impossible
To close the distance.
I can no more cross this room
Than Zeno's arrow.

A Policeman's Lot

The progress of any writer is marked by those moments when he
manages to outwit his own inner police system.   Ted Hughes

Oh, once I was a policeman young and merry (young and merry),
Controlling crowds and fighting petty crime (petty crime),
But now I work on matters literary (litererry)
And I am growing old before my time ('fore my time).
No, the imagination of a writer (of a writer)
Is not the sort of beat a chap would choose (chap would choose)
And they've assigned me a prolific blighter ('lific blighter) –
I'm patrolling the unconscious of Ted Hughes.

It's not the sort of beat a chap would choose (chap would
                                              choose) –
Patrolling the unconscious of Ted Hughes.

All our leave was cancelled in the lambing season (lambing
season),
When bitter winter froze the drinking trough (drinking trough),
For our commander stated, with good reason (with good reason),
That that's the kind of thing that starts him off (starts him off).
But anything with four legs causes trouble (causes trouble) –
It's worse than organizing several zoos (several zoos),
Not to mention mythic creatures in the rubble (in the rubble),
Patrolling the unconscious of Ted Hughes.

It's worse than organizing several zoos (several zoos) –
Patrolling the unconscious of Ted Hughes.

Although it's disagreeable and stressful (bull and stressful)
Attempting to avert poetic thought ('etic thought),
I could boast of times when I have been successful (been
successful)
And conspiring compound epithets were caught ('thets were
caught).
But the poetry statistics in this sector (in this sector)
Are enough to make a copper turn to booze (turn to booze)
And I do not think I'll make it to inspector (to inspector)
Patrolling the unconscious of Ted Hughes.

It's enough to make a copper turn to booze (turn to booze) –
Patrolling the unconscious of Ted Hughes.

after W. S. Gilbert

Waste Land Limericks

I

In April one seldom feels cheerful;
Dry stones, sun and dust make me fearful;
Clairvoyantes distress me,
Commuters depress me –
Met Stetson and gave him an earful.

II

She sat in a mighty fine chair,
Sparks flew as she tidied her hair;
She asks many questions,
I make few suggestions –
Bad as Albert and Lil – what a pair!

III

The Thames runs, bones rattle, rats creep;
Tiresias fancies a peep –
A typist is laid,
A record is played –
Wei la la. After this it gets deep.

IV

A Phoenician called Phlebas forgot
About birds and his business – the lot,
Which is no surprise
Since he'd met his demise
And been left in the ocean to rot.

WENDY COPE

V

No water. Dry rocks and dry throats,
Then thunder, a shower of quotes
From the Sanskrit and Dante.
Da. Damyata. Shantih.
I hope you'll make sense of the notes.

SELIMA HILL

Below Hekla

I appear like a bird from nowhere.
I have a new name.
I am as clean as a whistle.
I beat the buttermilk in big white bowls
until it is smooth.
I wash the pearly plates under the tap,
and fifty canvas bumpers and fifty socks.
They drip in the sun
below grey mountains like the moon's.

Each night I lift the children
in their sleep and hold out
the china pot for them:
Wilt þú pissa, elskan,
pissa, pissa I whisper
as I tiptoe from bed to bed . . .
Around mid-night,
I go to the geyser below Hekla
and bathe in the warm water.

I am a short fat English girl.
I am twenty-five mothers.
I lead my children in a line
across the heather to the church.
The father watches me
from his dark door.
He shakes his head,
and takes me by the hand:
Blessa þú, elskan, blessa þú!

And now, September,
dust is flying: the bus is here.
I am ready.
I am on my way to Reykjavik,
Leith, Liverpool . . .
The children of the Barnaheimilið
are running to the gate like hens.
Good-bye, blessa þú,
give our love to the Beatles, good-bye.

A Voice in the Garden

Gerald's here! my mother called,
Are you ready? The taxi was waiting
to take us to our weekly swimming lessons.
I drove through Marylebone like a VIP
our kind neighbour close beside me,
smelling of soap and peppermint . . .
He squatted on the edge of the pool
and shouted *One, two! One, two!* as I struggled
with the water like a kitten. I kept my eyes
on the gold buttons of his blazer.
They were as smooth and glossy
as the boiled sweets he liked to suck,
and offer to his young friends.
I sank and kicked and spat out water.
The bright buttons rose and fell . . .

And then one day he came in beside me,
his old grey body quaking
like a mollusc without its shell.
The wet wool of his bathing trunks
reminded me of blankets I had peed on.
His hands in the moving water
seemed to float between my legs.

[303]

He smiled. I swam to the edge of the pool
and pulled myself over the steps.
The heated water trickled down my legs
as I wrapped my towel round me, like a shawl.
That was our last swimming lesson,
but he still came to tea on Sundays,
after his 'little siesta',
and sat down in the seat next to mine.

As he listened to my mother –
picking his biscuits off his plate
with pink eager fingers, lifting
his tea-cup to his lips, and nodding –
he pressed a silver florin in my hand.
I kept them in a muff in my drawer,
under my uniform. At last I poured them
into a plastic bag and took them by bus
to The Little Sisters Of The Poor
in Albert Street . . . Next Sunday, I hid
in the garden, but he came pushing his way
through the roses, looking for me.
I heard the twigs breaking up, and his voice
in the bushes calling and calling –
Yoo-hoo, Gerald's here, yoo-hoo . . .

Biographical Notes

FLEUR ADCOCK   Born 1934, in New Zealand; has lived in England since 1963. Her *Selected Poems* were published by Oxford University Press in 1983.

MARGARET ATWOOD   Born 1939. Canadian poet, novelist and critic; has received numerous awards for her writing. Recent collections of poetry include: *Selected Poems*, Simon and Schuster, 1976; *Two-Headed Poems*, Oxford University Press, 1978; *True Stories*, Jonathan Cape, 1982.

MARGARET AVISON   Born 1918. Canadian. Received Governor-General's Award for Poetry, 1961. Recent publications: *The Dumbfounding*, Norton, 1966, and *Sunblue*, Lancelot Press, 1978.

ELIZABETH BARTLETT   Born 1924. British. Her books of poems are: *A Lifetime of Dying: Poems 1942–1979*, 1979, and *Strange Territory*, 1983, both published by Harry Chambers/Peterloo Poets.

PATRICIA BEER   Born 1924. British poet, critic and novelist; born and brought up in Devon. Recent publications include: *Selected Poems*, 1979, and *The Lie of the Land*, 1983, both published by Hutchinson.

FRANCES BELLERBY   1899–1975. British; lived mostly in Cornwall and Devon. Her *Selected Poems* were published in 1970, and *The First-Known* in 1975, both by Enitharmon Press.

CONNIE BENSLEY   Born 1929. British. Her two books of poems are: *Progress Report*, 1981, and *Moving In*, 1984, both published by Harry Chambers/Peterloo Poets.

MARY URSULA BETHELL 1874–1945. A New Zealander, but spent some years in Britain and Europe. Her *Collected Poems* were published by Oxford University Press in 1985.

ELIZABETH BISHOP 1911–1979. American. Born in Massachusetts; brought up largely by grandparents in Nova Scotia; later travelled widely and settled in Brazil. Her *Complete Poems 1927–1979* were published in New York by Farrar, Straus and Giroux and in London by Chatto & Windus, 1983.

LOUISE BOGAN 1897–1970. American poet and critic; for many years poetry editor of *The New Yorker*. Her major collections are: *Collected Poems, 1923–1953*, Noonday Press, 1954, and *The Blue Estuaries: Poems 1923–1968*, Farrar, Straus and Giroux, 1968.

EAVAN BOLAND Born 1945. Irish. Collections of poetry include: *The War Horse*, Gollancz, 1975; *In Her Own Image*, 1980, and *Night Feed*, 1982, both published by Arlen House.

GWENDOLYN BROOKS Born 1917. Black American poet. Awarded the Pulitzer Prize for Poetry, 1950, and many subsequent awards. Lives in Chicago. Recent publications include: *The World of Gwendolyn Brooks*, Harper & Row, 1971, and *To Disembark*, Third World Press, 1981.

EILÉAN NI CHUILLEANÁIN Born 1942. Irish. Books of poetry include: *Acts and Monuments*, 1972, *Site of Ambush*, 1975, and *The Second Voyage*, 1977, all published by Gallery Books, Dublin.

AMY CLAMPITT Born 1920. American. Her collections of poetry are: *The Kingfisher*, Knopf, 1983, and Faber and Faber, 1984; *What the Light Was Like*, Knopf, 1985, and Faber and Faber, 1986.

GILLIAN CLARKE Born 1937. British; has spent most of her life in South Wales. Her books of poetry are: *The Sundial*, Gower Press, 1978; *Letter from a Far Country*, Carcanet Press, 1982, and *Selected Poems*, Carcanet Press, 1985.

JANE COOPER   Born 1924. American; lives and teaches in New York. Her first collection, *The Weather of Six Mornings*, received the Lamont Award of the Academy of American Poets in 1968. Her most recent book is: *Scaffolding: New and Selected Poems*, Anvil Press, 1984.

WENDY COPE   Born 1945. British; lives in London. Her first full-length collection of poems is: *Making Cocoa for Kingsley Amis*, Faber and Faber, 1986.

FRANCES CORNFORD   1886–1960. British. Granddaughter of Charles Darwin; lived in Cambridge; five children. Publications include: *Collected Poems*, 1954, and *On a Calm Shore*, 1960, both published by Cresset Press.

ELIZABETH DARYUSH   1887–1977. British; daughter of the poet Robert Bridges. Her *Collected Poems* were published by Carcanet Press in 1976.

ROSEMARY DOBSON   Born 1920. Australian. Her *Selected Poems* were published by Angus & Robertson in 1973.

FREDA DOWNIE   Born 1929. British. Her chief publications are: *A Stranger Here*, 1977, and *Plainsong*, 1981, both published by Secker & Warburg.

LAURIS EDMOND   Born 1924. A New Zealander; lives in Wellington. Her *Selected Poems* were published by Oxford University Press in 1984.

U. A. FANTHORPE   Born 1929. British. Her first three collections of poetry are: *Side Effects*, 1978, *Standing To*, 1982, and *Voices Off*, 1984, all published by Harry Chambers/Peterloo Poets. Her *Collected Poems* were published by Penguin Books in 1986.

ELAINE FEINSTEIN Born 1930. British poet and novelist. Born in Lancashire, of Russian-Jewish parents. Her books of poetry include: *Some Unease and Angels: Selected Poems*, Hutchinson, 1977.

TESS GALLAGHER Born 1943. American. Recent publications are: *Instructions to the Double*, 1976, *Under Stars*, 1978, and *Willingly*, 1984, all published by Graywolf Press.

LOUISE GLÜCK Born 1943. American. Her collections of poetry are: *The Firstborn*, Anvil Press, 1969; *The House on Marshland*, Ecco Press, 1975, and Anvil Press, 1976; *Descending Figure*, Ecco Press, 1980.

BARBARA GUEST Born 1920. American. Recent publications include: *Moscow Mansions*, Viking Press, 1973; *The Countess from Minneapolis*, Burning Deck, 1976.

H.D. (born Hilda Doolittle) 1886–1961. American poet and novelist. Born in Pennsylvania; later lived in London (where she was associated with Pound and the Imagists, and briefly married to Richard Aldington) and in Switzerland. Her many volumes of poetry include: *Collected Poems 1912–1944*, Carcanet Press, 1984; *Helen in Egypt*, New Directions, 1961; *Hermetic Definition*, New Directions, 1972.

GWEN HARWOOD Born 1920. Australian; born in Brisbane; has taught music and been a church organist; now lives in Tasmania. Recent publications are: *Selected Poems*, Angus & Robertson, 1975; *The Lion's Bride*, Angus & Robertson, 1981.

SELIMA HILL Born 1945. British. Her first collection of poems is: *Saying Hello at the Station*, Chatto & Windus, 1984.

MOLLY HOLDEN 1927–1981. British. Her publications include: *Air and Chill Earth*, 1971, and *The Country Over*, 1975, both published by Chatto & Windus.

ROBIN HYDE (born Iris Guiver Wilkinson) 1906–1939. New Zealand novelist, journalist and poet. Travelled through China during the war with Japan in 1938, arrived in England ill, and committed suicide in 1939. Her *Selected Poems* were published by Oxford University Press in 1984.

ELIZABETH JENNINGS Born 1926. British. Her many collections of poetry include: *Collected Poems*, Macmillan, 1970; and *Selected Poems*, 1979, *Moments of Grace*, 1979, and *Celebrations and Elegies*, 1982, all published by Carcanet Press.

JUNE JORDAN Born 1936. Black American poet; lives in New York. Her publications include: *Things that I Do in the Dark: Selected Poetry*, Random House, 1977.

JENNY JOSEPH Born 1932. British. Recent collections are: *Rose in the Afternoon*, J. M. Dent, 1974; and *The Thinking Heart*, 1978, and *Beyond Descartes*, 1983, both published by Secker & Warburg.

MAXINE KUMIN Born 1925. American; born in Philadelphia; has received many literary awards, including a Pulitzer Prize, 1973. Recent collections are: *House, Bridge, Fountain, Gate*, Viking Press, 1975; *The Retrieval System*, Penguin Books, 1978; *Our Ground Time Here Will be Brief*, Viking Press, 1982.

DENISE LEVERTOV Born 1923. British-born, of a Russian-Jewish father and a Welsh mother. Moved to the US in 1948. Her many books of poetry include: *Collected Earlier Poems 1940–1960*, 1979, and *Poems 1960–1967*, 1983 (both published by New Directions, as were seven other collections) and *Selected Poems*, Bloodaxe Books, 1986.

GWENDOLYN MacEWEN Born 1941. Canadian poet, playwright and novelist. Received the Governor-General's Award for poetry, 1970. Recent collections are: *Magic Animals: Selected Poetry*, Macmillan, 1974; *Earthlight: Selected Poetry*, General Publishing Company, 1982; *The T. E. Lawrence Poems*, Mosaic Press, 1982.

SANDRA McPHERSON Born 1943. American. Collections of poetry include: *The Year of Our Birth*, Ecco Press, 1978, and *Patron Happiness*, Ecco Press, 1984.

CHARLOTTE MEW 1869–1928. British. Lived mostly in London and was published by Harold Monro's Poetry Bookshop. In 1928, alone after her sister's death and afraid of becoming insane, she committed suicide. Her poems are in: *Collected Poems and Prose*, edited by Val Warner, Virago/Carcanet Press, 1982.

JOSEPHINE MILES 1911–1985. American poet, scholar and critic. Born in Chicago; disabled by illness from childhood; became University Professor of English, emerita, at the University of California at Berkeley. Her ten volumes of poetry include: *Collected Poems, 1930–1983*, University of Illinois Press, 1983.

EDNA ST VINCENT MILLAY 1892–1950. American. Born in Maine; lived mostly in New York; achieved a widespread and precocious reputation for her poetry. Her *Collected Poems* were published in 1956 by Harper & Row.

ELMA MITCHELL Born 1919. British. Born in Scotland; now lives in Somerset. Her books of poetry are: *The Poor Man in the Flesh*, 1976, *The Human Cage*, 1979, and *Furnished Rooms*, 1983, all published by Harry Chambers/Peterloo Poets.

MARIANNE MOORE 1887–1972. American; born in St Louis, Missouri; later lived in New York. Received many awards and honours for her poetry. Her *Complete Poems* were published in New York by the Viking Press, 1967, and in London by Faber and Faber, 1968 (revised edition 1984).

LORINE NIEDECKER 1903–1970. American. Born and spent her life in Wisconsin. Her publications include: *Blue Chicory*, The Elizabeth Press, 1970; *My Life by Water: Collected Poems, 1936–1968*, Fulcrum Press, 1970.

[310]

P. K. PAGE Born 1917. Canadian. Received the Governor-General's Award for Poetry, 1954. Recent publications include: *Poems Selected and New*, Anansi Press, 1974; *Evening Dance of the Grey Flies*, Oxford University Press, 1981.

RUTH PITTER Born 1897. British. Awarded the Queen's Gold Medal for Poetry, 1955; Companion of Honour, 1974. Poems collected as: *Poems 1926–1966*, Barrie and Rockliff/Cresset Press, 1968 (published in New York as: *Collected Poems*, Macmillan, 1969); her latest book is *End of Drought*, Barrie and Jenkins, 1975.

SYLVIA PLATH 1932–1963. American. Born in Boston; later lived in England, where she married the poet Ted Hughes and had two children; committed suicide in 1963. Her *Collected Poems* were published by Faber and Faber in 1981.

ADRIENNE RICH Born 1929. American. Well known for her feminist writings as well as her poetry. The latest of her many volumes of poetry is: *The Fact of a Doorframe: Poems Selected and New, 1954–84*, Norton, 1984.

JUDITH RODRIGUEZ (née Green) Born 1936. Australian. Her collections of poetry include: *Nu-Plastik Fanfare Red, 1973*, and *Water Life, 1976*, both published by University of Queensland Press.

MURIEL RUKEYSER 1913–1980. American. Her many books of poetry include: *Collected Poems*, McGraw Hill, 1979.

CAROL RUMENS Born 1944. British; lives in London. Her publications include: *Unplayed Music*, 1981, and *Star Whisper*, 1983, both from Secker & Warburg, and *Direct Dialling*, Chatto & Windus, 1985.

E. J. SCOVELL Born 1907. British. Her books of poetry include: *The River Steamer*, Cresset Press, 1956, and *The Space Between*, Secker & Warburg, 1982.

EDITH SITWELL 1887–1964. British. A well-known and controversial figure for much of her life. Her *Collected Poems* were published by Macmillan in 1957.

STEVIE SMITH 1902–1971. British poet and novelist. Lived in London and worked as a secretary in a publishing firm. Awarded the Queen's Gold Medal for Poetry, 1969. Her *Collected Poems* were published by Penguin Books, 1985.

ANNE STEVENSON Born 1933, in England, of American parents; brought up in the US; now lives in England. Recent publications are: *Enough of Green*, 1977; *Minute by Glass Minute*, 1982; *The Fiction-Makers*, 1985, all published by Oxford University Press.

MAY SWENSON Born 1919. American, born in Logan, Utah; lives in New York; many awards and fellowships. Her publications include: *New and Selected Things Taking Place*, Little, Brown, 1978.

ANNE SZUMIGALSKI Born 1926, in England, but emigrated to Canada in 1951. Her latest book of poems is: *Doctrine of Signatures*, Fifth House, 1983.

JEAN VALENTINE Born 1934. American; born in Chicago; lives in New York. Publications include: *Dream Barker and Other Poems*, Yale University Press, 1965; *Pilgrims*, 1969, *Ordinary Things*, 1974, and *The Messenger*, 1979, all published by Farrar, Straus and Giroux.

ELLEN BRYANT VOIGT Born 1943. American; lives in Vermont. Her books of poems are: *Claiming Kin*, Wesleyan University Press, 1976, and *The Forces of Plenty*, Norton, 1983.

SYLVIA TOWNSEND WARNER 1893–1978. British novelist, poet, short story writer and musicologist. Her *Collected Poems*, including much previously unpublished or uncollected work, were published in 1982 by Carcanet Press and the Viking Press.

ANNA WICKHAM (born Edith Alice Mary Harper) 1884–1947. British; spent some of her youth in Australia but most of her adult life in London. Her poems were published by Harold Monro's Poetry Bookshop and in the US, and widely anthologized. They are collected in: *The Writings of Anna Wickham: Free Woman and Poet*, Virago, 1984.

JUDITH WRIGHT Born 1915. Australian. Well known for her conservationist activities as well as her poetry. Her publications include: *Collected Poems 1942–1970*, 1971, *Alive: Poems 1971–72*, 1973, and *Fourth Quarter*, 1976, all published by Angus & Robertson.

ELINOR WYLIE 1885–1928. American. Born into high society, famous in her lifetime for her beauty as well as her poetry, and notorious for her 'scandalous' sexual involvements. Her *Collected Poems* (1932) were reprinted by Knopf in 1966.

Index of Titles

Index of First Lines

[318]

Acknowledgements

For permission to reprint copyright material the publishers
gratefully acknowledge the following:

'The Ex-queen among the Astronomers' and 'Blue Glass' from
Selected Poems by Fleur Adcock (1983), © Fleur Adcock 1983,
reprinted by permission of Oxford University Press; 'Game after
Supper', 'Habitation' and 'Women Skating' from *Procedures from
Underground* by Margaret Atwood, published by Little, Brown
and Company, copyright 1970, published in Canada by Oxford
University Press Canada, copyright 1970; 'Siren Song' from *You
Are Happy*, published by Harper & Row Publishers, Inc., ©
Margaret Atwood 1974, reprinted by permission of the publishers
and Margaret Atwood; poems by Margaret Avison from *The
Dumbfounding*, reprinted by permission of W. W. Norton and
Company, Inc., copyright © 1966 by Margaret Avison; poems by
Elizabeth Bartlett were first published in *Strange Territory*
(Peterloo Poets, 1983), reprinted by permission of the author;
poems by Patricia Beer are taken from *Selected Poems* by Patricia
Beer, reprinted by permission of Hutchinson, an imprint of
Century Hutchinson Publishing Limited; 'A Clear Shell' from
Selected Poems (Enitharmon Press, 1970) and 'Bereaved Child's
First Night' from *The First-Known and Other Poems* (Enitharmon
Press, 1975), both by Frances Bellerby; 'Desires' first published in
Progress Report (Harry Chambers/Peterloo Poets, 1981) and
'Charity' first published in *Moving In* (Harry Chambers/Peterloo
Poets, 1984) are reprinted by permission of the author, Connie
Bensley, and Harry Chambers/Peterloo Poets; poems by Mary
Ursula Bethell are from *Collected Poems*, reprinted by permission
of Oxford University Press; poems by Elizabeth Bishop are
reprinted from *The Complete Poems, 1927–1979* by Elizabeth
Bishop, copyright © 1936, 1940, 1941, 1944, 1948, 1949, 1952,
1955, 1956, 1959, 1961, 1971, 1972 by Elizabeth Bishop, copyright
renewed © 1974, 1976 by Elizabeth Bishop, copyright © 1983 by
Alice Helen Methfessel, reprinted by permission of Farrar, Straus
and Giroux, Inc. A number of poems originally appeared in *The
New Yorker*; poems by Louise Bogan are from *The Blue Estuaries*
by Louise Bogan, copyright © 1968 by Louise Bogan, reprinted
by permission of Farrar, Straus and Giroux, Inc.; 'The Famine Road'

ACKNOWLEDGEMENTS

from *The War Horse* by Eavan Bolan, reprinted by permission of
the author and Arlen House Women's Press; poems by
Gwendolyn Brooks from *Selected Poems*, originally published by
Harper & Row (1963), reprinted by permission of the author;
poems by Eiléan Ni Chuilleanáin from *Acts and Monuments*
(1972) by Eiléan Ni Chuilleanáin, reprinted by permission of the
Gallery Press; 'Beach Glass', copyright © 1983 by Amy
Clampitt, 'A Procession at Candlemas', copyright © 1981 by
Amy Clampitt, both reprinted from *The Kingfisher*, by permission
of Alfred A. Knopf, Inc. and Faber & Faber Limited; 'What the
Light Was Like' from *What the Light Was Like* by Amy Clampitt,
copyright © 1985 by Amy Clampitt, reprinted by permission
of Alfred A. Knopf, Inc. and Faber & Faber Limited; 'Baby-
sitting' from *The Sundial* by Gillian Clarke (Gomer Press, 1978);
'a poem with capital letters', copyright 1948 by Jane Cooper,
'My Young Mother', copyright 1964 by Jane Cooper, 'El Sueño
de la Razón', copyright © 1967 by Jane Cooper, all from *Maps
& Windows* by Jane Cooper, reprinted by permission of Macmillan
Publishing Company; 'Dispossessions' from *Maps & Windows* by
Jane Cooper, copyright © 1973 by Jane Cooper, reprinted by
permission of Macmillan Publishing Company (originally printed
in *The American Poetry Review*); all poems by Jane Cooper printed
in UK and Commonwealth from *Scaffolding*, copyright © 1984
by Jane Cooper, reprinted by permission of Anvil Press Poetry;
'Depression' by Wendy Cope from *Poetry Introduction 5* (Faber,
1982), all other poems from *Making Cocoa for Kingsley Amis* (Faber,
1986); all poems by Frances Cornford from *Collected Poems* (1954)
by Frances Cornford (Cresset Press, an imprint of Century
Hutchinson); 'Still-Life' from *Collected Poems* (1976) by Elizabeth
Daryush, reprinted by permission of the author and Carcanet Press
Limited; poems by Rosemary Dobson from *Selected Poems* by
Rosemary Dobson, copyright © Rosemary Dobson, 1973,
reprinted by permission of Angus & Robertson Publishers;
'Great-grandfather' and 'Her Garden' from *A Stranger Here* and
'Miss Grant' and 'Starlight' from *Plainsong*, both by Freda Downie,
reprinted by permission of the author and Secker and Warburg
Limited; 'A Difficult Adjustment' from *Selected Poems* (1984) by
Lauris Edmond, reprinted by permission of the author and Oxford
University Press, 'The Sums' (*PN Review*, 1985), reprinted by
permission of the author; 'Not My Best Side' by U. A. Fanthorpe,
first published in *Side Effects* (Peterloo Poets, 1978) and 'At the

ACKNOWLEDGEMENTS

Ferry', 'Resuscitation Team' and 'Father in the Railway Buffet'
first published in *Standing To* (Peterloo Poets, 1982); 'Lais' from
The Celebrants (1973) and 'Patience' from *Some Unease and Angels*
(1977) both by Elaine Feinstein, reprinted by permission of
Hutchinson, an imprint of Century Hutchinson, and the author;
'Instructions to the Double' is from *Instructions to the Double* by
Tess Gallagher (Graywolf Press, Washington, 1976), other
poems from *Willingly* (Graywolf Press, Washington, 1984); 'For
Jane Myers', 'Gratitude' and 'The Undertaking' from *The House
on the Marshland* by Louise Glück, copyright 1974 by Louise
Glück (The Ecco Press, 1975), reprinted by permission of the
publishers; 'Descending Figure', 'Dedication to Hunger' and 'The
Gift' from *Descending Figure* by Louise Glück, copyright © 1980 by
Louise Glück (The Ecco Press, 1980), reprinted by permission;
poems by Barbara Guest are from *Moscow Mansions* by Barbara
Guest, copyright © 1973 by Barbara Guest, reprinted by
permission of Viking Penguin, Inc.; 'Helen', 'Lethe' and extract
from 'Sigil' from *Collected Poems* (1984) by H. D. (Hilda Doolittle),
reprinted by permission of the author and Carcanet Press
Limited, published in the United States by New Directions
Publishing Corporation, copyright © 1982 by the Estate of Hilda
Doolittle; extract from 'Winter Love' from *Hermetic Definition* by
H. D., copyright © 1972 by Norman Holmes Pearson; 'Hospital
Evening' from *Selected Poems*, 'In the Bistro' from *Poems/Volume 2*
and 'A Simple Story', an extract from 'A Quartet for Dorothy
Hewett', from *The Lion's Bride*, all by Gwen Harwood, copyright
© Gwen Harwood 1975, 1968, 1981, reprinted by permission of
Angus & Robertson (UK) Limited; poems by Selima Hill from
Saying Hello at the Station by Selima Hill, reprinted by permission
of the author and Chatto & Windus; 'Seaman, 1941', originally
from *Air and Chill Earth* by Molly Holden (Chatto & Windus,
1971), sole copyright, Alan Holden; extract from 'The Beaches' by
Robin Hyde from *Selected Poems* (Oxford University Press, New
Zealand, 1984), reprinted by permission of the Executor, Derek
Challis; 'Fragment for the Dark' from *Consequently I Rejoice* by
Elizabeth Jennings, (Carcanet, 1977); 'One Flesh' from *Collected
Poems* by Elizabeth Jennings (Macmillan, 1967); poems by June
Jordan from *Things That I Do in the Dark* by June Jordan, reprinted
by permission of Beacon Press; 'Warning' from *Rose in the
Afternoon* by Jenny Joseph (Dent, 1974); poems by Maxine Kumin
from *Our Ground Time Here Will be Brief* by Maxine Kumin,

copyright © 1973, 1976 by Maxine Kumin, reprinted by
permission of Viking Penguin Inc.; 'Matins' and 'Abel's Bride' by
Denise Levertov from *Poems: 1960–1967* by Denise Levertov,
copyright © 1961 by Denise Levertov Goodman, reprinted by
permission of New Directions Publishing Corporation, and
'Goethe's Blues' from *Footprints* by Denise Levertov, copyright ©
1972 by Denise Levertov, first published in the *North American
Review*; 'Sea Things' from *Magic Animals* and 'You Cannot Do
This' from *Earthlight*, both by Gwendolyn MacEwen, reprinted by
permission of the author and Stoddart Publishing Company
Limited, Toronto, Canada, and 'The Virgin Warrior' from *The T. E.
Lawrence Poems* by Gwendolyn MacEwen, published by Mosaic
Press, Oakville, Ontario, Canada, copyright 1983, reprinted by
permission of the publisher; '1943' and 'Children' © 1978 by
Sandra McPherson from *The Year of Our Birth* by Sandra
McPherson, published by The Ecco Press in 1978, reprinted by
permission; poems by Charlotte Mew from *Collected Poems and
Prose* (1982), reprinted by permission of the author and Carcanet
Press Limited; 'Conception', 'Family', 'Album' and 'Officers' by
Josephine Miles from *Collected Poems, 1930–1983*, (University of
Illinois Press, 1983), 'The Day the Winds', 'Summer', 'Belief',
'Ride' and 'Bibliographer' by Josephine Miles from *Prefabrications*
(Indiana University Press); poems by Edna St Vincent Millay from
Collected Poems by Edna St Vincent Millay, Harper & Row,
copyright © 1921, 1922, 1931, 1934, 1948, 1950 by Edna St Vincent
Millay, copyright © 1954, 1958, 1962 by Norma Millay Ellis,
reprinted by permission; 'Thoughts After Ruskin' by Elma
Mitchell, first published in *The Poor Man in the Flesh* (Peterloo
Poets, 1976); 'The Steeple-Jack', copyright © 1951 by Marianne
Moore, renewed 1979 by Lawrence E. Brinn and Louise Crane,
'Spenser's Ireland' copyright © 1941, renewed 1969 by Marianne
Moore, 'I May, I might, I must', 'The Jerboa', 'The Fish', 'Poetry',
'Critics and Connoisseurs', 'England', 'A Grave', 'To a Snail',
'Silence', 'The Pangolin', 'The Paper Nautilus', copyright © 1935
by Marianne Moore, renewed 1963 by Marianne Moore and T. S.
Eliot, all from *Collected Poems* by Marianne Moore, reprinted with
permission of Macmillan Publishing Company and Faber and
Faber Limited; 'Lake Superior' from *The Granite Pal* by Lorine
Niedecker, copyright © 1985 by the Estate of Lorine Niedecker,
Cid Corman, Executor, published by the North Point Press and
reprinted by permission; 'Brazilian Fazenda' from *Poems Selected*

and New (1974) by P. K. Page, reprinted by permission of the author; poems by Ruth Pitter from *Poems 1926–1966* (1968) by Ruth Pitter (Cresset Press, an imprint of Century Hutchinson); poems by Sylvia Plath from *Collected Poems* (1981) edited by Ted Hughes, poems copyright © the Estate of Sylvia Plath, 1960, 1965, 1971, 1981; poems by Adrienne Rich from *The Fact of a Doorframe, Poems Selected and New, 1950–1984* by Adrienne Rich, reprinted by permission of W. W. Norton and Company, Inc. copyright © 1975, 1978 by W. W. Norton, copyright © 1981 by Adrienne Rich, copyright © 1984 by Adrienne Rich; 'The Handloom' from *Nu-Plastik Fanfare Red and Other Poems* by Judith Rodriguez (University of Queensland Press, 1973), 'How Come the Truck-loads?', 'Eskimo Occasion' from *Water Life* by Judith Rodriguez (University of Queensland Press, 1976); 'Then I Saw What the Calling Was', 'Myth' from *Collected Poems* by Muriel Rukeyser (McGraw Hill, 1978), reprinted by permission of International Creative Management; poems by Carol Rumens from *Star Whisper* by Carol Rumens (Secker and Warburg, 1983); poems by E. J. Scovell from *Shadows of Chrysanthemums* (Routledge and Kegan Paul, 1944); 'Sir Beelzebub' from *Collected Poems* by Edith Sitwell (Macmillan, 1957); poems by Stevie Smith from *The Collected Poems*, copyright © 1972 by Stevie Smith, reprinted by permission of the New Directions Publishing Corporation (USA) and of the Executor, James MacGibbon; 'By the Boat House, Oxford' from *Enough of Green* (1977) by Anne Stevenson, © Anne Stevenson 1977, and 'Himalayan Balsam', 'Suicide' and 'Giving Rabbit to my Cat Bonnie' from *Minute by Glass Minute* by Anne Stevenson (1982), © Anne Stevenson 1982, reprinted by permission of Oxford University Press; 'The Centaur' by May Swenson, copyright © 1956, 1984 by May Swenson, 'The James Bond Movie' by May Swenson, copyright © 1968 by May Swenson, both poems originally from *New and Selected Things Taking Place* (Little, Brown, 1978), reprinted by permission of the author; poems by Anne Szumigalski from *Doctrine of Signatures* (Fifth House, 1983); 'Orpheus and Eurydice' from *Pilgrims* by Jean Valentine, copyright © 1967, 1969 by Jean Valentine, reprinted by permission of Farrar, Straus and Giroux, Inc., 'A Bride's Hours' and 'Sex' from *Dream Barker and Other Poems* by Jean Valentine, reprinted by permission of Yale University Press; 'Why She Says No' from *The Forces of Plenty* by Ellen Bryant Voigt, reprinted by permission of W. W. Norton and

ACKNOWLEDGEMENTS

Company, Inc., copyright © 1983 by Ellen Bryant Voigt;
'Gloriana Dying' from *Twelve Poems* by Sylvia Townsend
Warner, reprinted by permission of the Estate of Sylvia
Townsend Warner and Chatto & Windus, The Hogarth Press;
'Now in this long-deferred spring' and 'King Duffus' from
Collected Poems (1982) by Sylvia Townsend Warner, reprinted
by permission of the author and Carcanet Press Limited; poems
by Anna Wickham from *The Writings of Anna Wickham* by
Anna Wickham, reprinted by permission of Virago Press and
the author; poems by Judith Wright from *Selected Poems* by
Judith Wright, copyright © Judith Wright 1963, reprinted by
permission of Angus & Robertson Publisher's; 'Prophecy',
copyright 1923 by Alfred A. Knopf, Inc. and renewed 1951 by
Edwina G. Rubenstein, and 'Wild Peaches', copyright 1921 by
Alfred A. Knopf, Inc. and renewed 1949 by William Rose
Benet, both reprinted from *The Collected Poems of Elinor Wylie*
by permission of Alfred A. Knopf, Inc.

The following poems first appeared in *The New Yorker*: 'The
Bight', 'At the Fishhouses', 'Arrival at Santos', 'Brazil, January 1,
1502', 'Manuelzinho', 'First Death in Nova Scotia', 'In the
Waiting Room' and 'The Moose' by Elizabeth Bishop; 'What
the Light Was Like' by Amy Clampitt; 'Black Silk' by Tess
Gallagher; 'Family' by Josephine Miles; 'The Moon and the Yew
Tree', 'Mirror' and 'Among the Narcissi' by Sylvia Plath.

Faber and Faber apologizes for any errors or omissions in the
above list and would be grateful to be notified of any
corrections that should be incorporated in the next edition of
this volume.